How & Why You Should Wait On GOD For Your Husband

Dedication

This book is dedicated to you, the woman of GOD who wants to please the LORD with her life and her body.

Introduction

How should you wait on GOD for your husband? Why should you wait on GOD for your husband? This is no ordinary single's book. This is a book that is going to compel you to rethink how you've viewed single life through:

- Wisdom
- Knowledge
- And My Testimony

Wisdom lovingly comes forward, ready to embrace the women of GOD, but many of them reject her. Therefore, she has to send forth Papa Wisdom, otherwise known as Experience. Experience carries the belt of truth, and Experience has left a wake of chastened women in his path. His goal, however, isn't to hurt you. His goal is to get you to reject sin so you can finally embrace the LORD.

I am a woman who has been beaten up by Experience. Having been twice married and twice divorced, GOD began to use me to speak with HIS daughters about what it means to get with the wrong men and what the consequences are. I'm not the woman who comes forth saying she's been happily married for twenty-plus years. Sure, she can teach you if you'll listen, but I'm the woman who comes forth to show you my scars so you can stop thinking there is a way around the WORD of GOD.

This powerful read will make you laugh, cry and rethink how you view relationships. GOD has your Mr. Right in store, but you've just got to stop settling for Mr. Right Now.

Table of Contents

Introduction..V

Twice Bitten, Never Loved 1

When is Mr. Right Coming?.................................35

Why Should I Wait?...55

Considering Your Options..................................67

How to Wait....Patiently...................................75

In the Meantime...83

She Got Married...You Didn't..............................93

50 Obvious Ishmaels to Avoid.............................101

Satan's Favorite Weapon..................................137

Be Anxious For Nothing...................................143

You're Worth the Wait....Is He?.........................151

Breaking Up With Mr. Wrong 169

Obedience is Better than Sacrifice.......................177

In Storage...189

The Importance of Identification.........................215

Secretly Single..227

Marrying Perception......................................239

Just Stop Waiting..251

His Story Repeats Itself.................................255

His Height...261

Lying to Yourself..273

Building a Solid Foundation..............................281

The Power of Your Testimony..............................293

Unplugged..313

Thinking Like a Wife.....................................321

Commonly Asked Questions.................................333

Scriptural Direction.....................................357

Twice Bitten, Never Loved

I looked in the mirror and saw the woman looking back at me. *I love me some me*, I thought to myself. What I didn't realize was that I was lying to myself. How could I love the woman looking back at me when I kept putting her in situations that endangered her life and her sanity? Nevertheless, I was only looking out for her, in my own warped mind. She had to go into the darkness and feel around for Mr. Right, and that meant she'd trip over a few snakes along the way. But when she found Mr. Right, he would be all so worth it. In my imagination, I would find or be found by the right man, but in order to be found, I had to go into places where men were looking. So, for a couple of years, a lost and wanted-to-be-found me went into one club after another. I was surrounded by women like myself, only I had a game plan. I'd wear the skimpiest clothes to show off my then slender figure, and I'd sort through the crowd of men who'd drool and hiss as we walked by. If I found one worth dating, I'd grab him by his collar and pull him to the dance floor. He would be my dancing partner for the evening, and if he played his cards right, he may be blessed to have a lifetime with me.

I dated and I dated....and I dated some more. I was so overly confident that I'd toss away any obvious Mr. Wrong without hesitation. I was proud to say I wasn't like my friends. I could toss them without a tear, and then I'd be out again, half-dressed and waiting for the next big nab. What I didn't realize was that I was broken, and my behavior towards men was the evidence of unsevered soul ties, unforgiveness and lack of knowledge.

It didn't matter how far I went into sin, GOD kept calling me to come out of it. In the public eye, I was confident and daring. At home, I found myself crying a lot because there was a war going on within the depths of my soul. It was a war for my soul, and Satan felt that he'd worked overtime making sure I was lost, perverted and hell-bound, so he didn't give up easily without a fight. After all the molestations I'd endured, the mental and physical abuse and the dysfunctional home I'd grown up in, there was no way he was letting me go without a fight. And fight he did; nevertheless, GOD would prevail as usual.

In 1999, I finally surrendered my life to the LORD, but not my mind. I didn't know the mind had to be changed. I just thought I'd get saved and everything else would fall into place. I went to church faithfully, and I was happy that I'd finally surrendered to GOD. I stopped going to the clubs, and I stopped getting intoxicated; nevertheless, I'd drink some sweet alcoholic beverages from time to time. I'd even stopped hanging out with many of the people I once partied with. I was serious about GOD, and I tried hard to turn my life around. Nevertheless, there were still a few things I felt I needed from sin, and once I got those things, I could turn my life all the way around back to GOD.

In the year 2000, I met the man who'd one day become my first husband. I was out with a friend and a cousin of mine, and we'd stopped by the local gas station to pick up some alcoholic beverages. We were going to be hanging out at my cousin's house with a bunch of his friends, and we planned to play cards and laugh the night away. I was always in search of fun because I didn't know what joy was. I met my first husband at that gas station, and we were pretty much inseparable from that moment on. Our relationship moved really fast. He was going through a divorce, and even though I was convicted in my heart, I convinced myself that I wasn't taking him from his wife. He was separated from his wife, and they'd already signed the divorce papers, so I felt that he was fair game. We ended up living together for two years before getting married. Of course, those two years were torturous because I often worried about my soul. After all, fornication is a sin, and I didn't want to go to hell because of it. That was my reason for trying to live right. I didn't want to go to hell.

After two years of shacking, he finally proposed, and I felt like I'd finally found the perfect bridge between sin and righteousness. In my mind, it had to be okay to sin if your plan was to make it right eventually.

Over the course of our marriage, I'd gotten closer to GOD, and I found that the closer I got to GOD, the further away I got from my husband. I started taking my walk with GOD more seriously, and I wanted to rid my life of every evil thing and every evil person in it. We'd argue a lot because I didn't like his friends or the people he liked to hang around with, and I'd pretty much stopped associating with most of the women I'd once called friends. I wanted saved friends, and I oftentimes fantasized about my husband being saved and us being surrounded by other people who loved the LORD.

During that marriage, he did many of the right things, but when he did wrong...he did it big. There were two problems that would eventually destroy our marriage: His inability to be faithful and his temper. Don't get me wrong, I had a temper too, but after losing a fight with him during our shacking phase, I'd learn to put my rage in check and keep my hands to myself. I'd probably hit him two times in the beginning of our courtship, but after that, I'd stopped. He didn't stop, however. Over the years, I found myself trying to fight him off me, running from him or trying to soothe him when he got angry. I'd even thought about killing or severely harming him when he'd attacked me a few times. I told myself that I wasn't being abused because I felt that I'd provoked him by arguing with him or because I'd gotten in his face a few times. I thought abuse was when the woman didn't fight back. In many of our brawls, I did fight back, but I could just never win the fight. The fights would always end with me pinned against the wall or lying on the floor with his hands tightly around my neck. I knew what that threat meant. It meant that the next stop was six feet under if I didn't stop squirming or fighting back. After each fight, I'd watch him pace back and forth, cursing, screaming and breaking things. I'd even called the police a few times. There was one time when he'd taken a belt and struck me repeatedly with it. I had defensive wounds on my arms from trying to stop the belt from striking my face, but the police told me that if I pressed charges on him, he could press charges on me. I was enraged because I hadn't done anything, and they were basically handing him a get-out-of-jail-free card so they wouldn't have to fill out any paperwork. I didn't press charges that day. Instead, I did what the police told me to do. I left and went to stay at a friend's house overnight. Those officers were later reprimanded when I'd reported what they'd done.

Along with his temper was his insatiable appetite for other women. One woman in particular decided that she would stalk me to get me to leave him. We were twenty-six years old, and this woman was forty-two years old. I didn't think he'd be attracted to someone sixteen years his senior, but after receiving so many calls from this woman, I had to face reality. My husband was having an affair with a woman I'd addressed as "ma'am."

Of course, it was only a matter of time before that marriage ended. While we were going through the divorce, I found myself struggling with a force I didn't know was present in my life. I found myself struggling with the very stronghold that held the women in my family captive. They didn't know how to live without having a man, and neither did I, so I began to surround myself with women: both lost and found. I didn't realize it then, but I was trying to silence the demons that had tormented my family for hundreds, or maybe thousands of years. I tried to muffle the sounds of my broken heart by always surrounding myself with people; nevertheless, I knew one sure-fire way to feel better, and that was to get into another relationship. It wouldn't heal my broken heart, but it would at least distract me while my heart healed...or so I thought.

Almost a year after my first husband and I separated, I met the man who would become my second ex-husband. He was living in Germany, and I was living back at my mother's house in Mississippi. I'd lost my home to foreclosure and lost my car to the bank. I was in a low place, but I was being built back up by GOD. You see, before I lost my home, the LORD spoke to me one day and told me that I was going to build a website. Being still somewhat young in the faith, I took that and ran with it in the wrong direction. What would I create a website about? What did I have that was marketable? I didn't wait on the LORD for my answer; I just went and created a website. I decided to create a website featuring hip hop artists and models. After all, I liked hip hop (at that time), and I wanted to involve myself in a world that involved people. And that's how I met my second husband. He came along because he'd seen my website and was interested in my site....and then me.

My second husband was in school in Germany, and my initial attraction to him wasn't a romantic one. He wasn't the type of man I'd ordinarily go for, but I was fascinated with him because he was foreign. He was from Cameroon, Africa; he was in school to be a bio-engineer, and he spoke five languages. I wanted to know about his country because I'd never been outside of my own country, let alone met an African before. Being from a small city in Mississippi, I hadn't met too many people from other countries because foreigners aren't usually attracted to Mississippi, since it's one of the lowest paying states in the United States.

After speaking with him for a while, I found myself becoming more and more attracted to him. After a while, I found myself wanting to be with him because I thought that maybe the problem was in American men. They obviously didn't know what they wanted, and here was this man who had no children and boasted on loving his family. He represented almost everything I wanted in a husband. All but one important thing: He did not love the LORD. Nevertheless, I thought I could change that. All I would have to do was tell him more and more about CHRIST and what HE'D done for me. He said he believed in the LORD, so that was a good start in my mind. After he made his interest in me known, I became his "girlfriend."

Jay and I talked for almost a year before we finally met, and after we met one another, we were both sold on each other. We wanted to get married immediately, but we couldn't because the divorce from my first marriage was still pending. I wanted to get married because I didn't want to be in fornication, or in my case, adultery. Once Jay and I crossed that line, I felt that horrible conviction come over me once again, and I did not want to be in wrong-standing with the LORD. Jay wanted to get married because he said it was "his time." He was almost thirty years old and in his last year of college, so in March of 2008, the divorce from my first husband was finalized and in April of 2008, Jay and I got married in Denmark. *I've finally done it*, I thought. I'd met the man I'd spend my life with. It was too bad he had to be a foreign man, but I felt that our cultures couldn't be too different to make a difference. I was wrong.

A woman Jay said was his sister lived in the United States, and he'd introduced me to her not long after we first met. She was about ten to fifteen years older than him, so

I didn't think too much about it. Little did I know that this woman would be a huge force that would challenge our marriage and make me lose almost every ounce of respect I had for Jay. We'll call her Mara. Mara told Jay that I was not to move to Germany with him. Instead, she wanted me to move to Georgia with her until Jay finished his thesis. Mara also told Jay and I that when we had our first child, we were to give that child to her, and she would raise the baby. She said that after giving her our first child, we could keep the rest of our children. Of course, I strongly opposed her requests and this started a fire between the two of us. What struck me as weird was that Jay was willing, however.

Once I moved to Germany with Jay, our problems continued. Jay wasn't a compassionate man, nor did he agree with my American way of thinking. Jay wanted to be married, but independent. He didn't like the idea of me going too many places with him, and he felt that I was out of line for demanding that he stopped talking with his ex-girlfriends as well as women he'd met here and there. He would often claim that he was no longer speaking with his exes, but Jay spoke French, so I didn't understand what he was saying or who he was saying it to. Our marriage became one of insecurity, hurt, betrayal and a huge lesson for me.

When we moved to the United States, the plan was to live with Jay's sister for a little over a month, which of course, I was passionately against. Every time we'd been to Mara's house in the past, we'd fought like we didn't know each other. Jay had never physically put his hands on me, but we'd argue viciously at Mara's house. We moved back to the United States in mid February of 2010, and Jay was supposed to start his new job in April of that year.

From the day we walked into her apartment, Mara refused to greet me. As with every other visit, she always tried to separate Jay from me. She'd given us her son's room to sleep in, so I spent most of my days in that room when she was not at work. If Jay came into the room with me, she'd scream his name until he went to where she was, or she'd come and beat on the door if it was locked. I was living in a nightmare.

In June of that year, Jay and I finally moved to Florida, and I thought the end of Mara's reign in his life was over. We'd purchased a cell phone, and we shared that phone until we could get on our feet. Mara continued to call that phone several times a day, and Jay and I fought daily about her intrusiveness. She told Jay:

- To never put me on his bank account, and he listened. He insisted that I have my own separate account.
- To get another bank account that I had no knowledge of, and he listened. I didn't find out until a couple of years later that he had a couple of secret accounts that he stored money in.
- To get a post office box that I had no knowledge of. She didn't like that I saw all of the mail going out and coming into our apartment. Of course, Jay listened.
- To get a car and not put my name on it. She said that I hadn't contributed a dime to that marriage; therefore, Jay was to buy the car and put it in his name.

- To force me to get a job so I could help him with the bills. He tried to, but I went before the LORD because I wanted to own my own business. By that time, I'd closed that hip hop site years ago at the urging of the LORD, and had now committed to working only with the Kingdom. GOD heard my prayer and immediately blessed me with my own business. It wasn't long before I was making more money than Jay.

I often repented, cried and begged the LORD to release me from the marriage I was in. By this time, I'd grown up in the LORD so much that GOD was using me to minister to HIS daughters as to why they should wait on HIM for their husbands. I had a friend back then who GOD used to shed some light into something that was going on in my heart;

something that was affecting GOD'S ministry in me. I was angry with myself for the sins I'd committed against the LORD. I had a love in me for HIM that had grown so much that I often beat myself up with my thoughts and basically told myself and others that I deserved everything I was going through. Why had I put myself in such a bad situation? I felt like I was stuck in that marriage and that my punishment would be me seeing other women who had waited get their Isaacs while I continued to suffer with Ahab and Jezebel. One day, while talking with my friend, I was going on and on about how I'd sinned against the LORD and how I was living in my payback. My friend said to me, "Tiffany, I have heard you speak on forgiveness a lot. You have forgiven your ex-husband and everyone who's hurt you, but the one person you forgot to forgive was yourself." My heart broke hearing those words. She was telling the truth. Of all the lessons I was teaching other women about waiting on GOD and forgiving the men in their past, the one lesson I'd missed out on was how to forgive myself. GOD had forgiven me, but I hadn't forgiven myself, so I constantly apologized to HIM and begged for HIS forgiveness.

Jay and I remained married for five years, and we had a few ups and plenty of downs. During the course of our marriage, GOD continued to grow me up and use me to minister to single and married women all across the world. I had to stop being ashamed of my testimony in order for me to tell it. I'd messed up, and I knew I'd messed up. The LORD told me that there were two types of women HE'D sent forth to minister to HIS daughters. There are the ones who'd done everything the right way, and then there were the ones like myself. The hard-headed ones who had to minister from a place of experience, and we were the ones HE sent to speak to HIS stubborn daughters. You see, most women who grew up in broken homes have trouble receiving counsel from women who grew up in good homes and led what looked like perfect lives. All that I'd been through hadn't been for nothing. Even though it wasn't GOD'S will for me to have been molested, misguided, raped, beaten, divorced, persecuted and judged, it had all happened, and GOD could still use it for HIS glory. GOD gave me the strength to endure because HE wanted to use me.

One day, while Jay and I were still together, I walked into my bathroom, and as I was washing my hands, I looked up at my reflection and began to cry. Here I was,

writing books and being used by the LORD
to help HIS daughters, but I felt helpless in
my own life. I felt sorry for myself. Would I
spend my life never knowing what it felt like
to be loved by a man? Before I could get a
good cry in, GOD said to me, "You're strong
enough." Suddenly, the tears wouldn't
come out. From that day forth, GOD started
teaching me how to be alone, even in the
midst of my marriage. My husband would
take many trips for his job and for Mara,
and he didn't want me to come with him.
He'd pacify me with a yearly cruise and by
accepting my request to dine out together
once a week. He would travel between six
to ten times a year, while I was left at home
for a week or two each trip. At first, I would
argue with him, and I would count down the
days until he came home. But once GOD
told me that HE was teaching me how to be
alone, I stopped arguing with Jay. I'd come

to expect his frequent trips; trips that he wouldn't tell me about until one to two days before his scheduled flights. I knew it was likely that he was having an affair, but I knew there was nothing I could do but wait on GOD for direction. I knew that our marriage would end, but the hard part was waiting for the green light from the LORD to get up and go. You see, when GOD tells you to go, HE opens up another door for you. I wanted to remain obedient this time. I didn't want to move in my own flesh. I wanted to specifically hear from GOD as to what I was to do.

During this time, I told GOD that if HE ever delivered me from Jay, I would wait on HIM for my husband. I would NEVER fornicate or commit adultery again. I now loved HIM enough to obey HIM. Years would go by, and I would deal with Jay's almost incestuous-like relationship with Mara. I felt helpless, stupid and low. I'd run out of lies to tell myself, and it was now time to face the whole truth. Jay and I would never grow old together. Jay and I would end up in divorce court because, even though the papers said he was married to me, it was obvious that his obligations were to Mara and his family.

I asked the LORD to deliver me or change Jay. Either way, I did not want the man I was married to. He wasn't compassionate; he didn't like spending time with me, and he didn't like talking with me but seemed obsessed with Mara. Every time a family member would call and talk about some crazy thing Mara had done, he'd chuckle lovingly, and I could tell he was fascinated with her ignorance. After all of the attacks against my marriage, I found myself hating

Mara, and then, I found myself beginning to secretly wish she'd die. Once I realized this, I confessed it to GOD and asked HIM to deliver me from that hatred. Over the course of time, I'd even began to despise my own husband. One day, I found myself telling him that I wished he'd get hit by a car. Another day, I told him that I wished he'd get stumped by an elephant whenever he visited Africa. I couldn't believe the words that I'd just spoken, and I repented of them immediately; nevertheless, this told me that I'd let the sun set on my wrath one too many times. I had to spend some time before the altar to be cleansed.

As I continued to minister to single women, I found that GOD was using me to minister to myself. I learned the lessons that I needed, and once Jay finally left me, I knew that GOD was blessing me with the opportunity to serve HIM the right way. HE was delivering me from a marriage full of hurt, lies and secrets. On one hand, I was relieved. On the other hand, I was hurt because I was losing a man I loved, despite his flaws. But I knew it was over, and I knew my life would get better from that day on out. I could now wait for Isaac and stop trying to teach Ishmael how to be Isaac.

My Reality
I am the woman GOD sends to you to speak of what it's like on the other side of wrong. I'd told a woman once to watch Juanita Bynum's "No More Sheets" video to help her with her single life. She responded by telling me that she could not listen to Juanita Bynum because Juanita had been married twice, so she could not take her advice. I smiled and responded to her, "That's why I would take Juanita's advice.

She knows where she went wrong, and women like her often preach from a place of having been delivered from the very things that other women will one day beg to be delivered from. Women like Juanita can stop you from making those mistakes."

I've learned what demons are, and I've learned about many of the devils that are out and about seeking to devour naïve and impatient Christian women. I went into sin, and I married the men I found there twice. This book isn't just going to guide you; it's going to rebuke you, question you, and cause you to go before the LORD with your concerns. I got delivered from the evils that once tried to destroy me from within. I survived myself. You don't have to end up with my testimony or a custom-created testimony fit for a fool in love. You could become a living testimony of what GOD can

and will do for a woman who serves HIM
with her mind, body, spirit and soul.

How did I forgive the men and their allies
for taking me through so much? I took
responsibility for my own actions. How
dare I point the fingers at them without
realizing that I'd done wrong too. I'd met
and married men who were in the world,
and I tried to drag them into the church. I'd
met men who were not even of the same
faith as I was, and I tried to lead them to
CHRIST. I'm a woman. I'm not created to
lead a man to CHRIST; I was created to be
led by my husband in CHRIST. I had more of
a responsibility in the failure of those
marriages than those men had. I didn't
want to admit it at first, but it's true. I'd
sinned to get them, and I'd placed them
before GOD. After that, I suddenly wanted
to change the dynamics of our marriages.

Sure, your spouse has to be second to GOD, but a worldly man won't accept that line-up, and I knew that, so I played musical chairs with GOD and my husbands. Over the course of those marriages, I found myself telling them about the LORD daily, hoping that they'd surrender to HIM. I was wrong in getting with them, and accepting that I was wrong helped me to forgive them. They weren't awful men. They had great things in them that made me fall in love with them initially. But it was the bad that drove me away, and it was my desire to serve the LORD that drove them away from me. Light and darkness cannot comprehend one another. "Be ye not unequally yoked together with unbelievers: for what fellowship hath righteousness with unrighteousness? And what communion hath light with darkness?" (2 Corinthians 6:14).

A woman who does not forgive a sinner for being a sinner is a woman who is too blind to see her own sin.

One thing you'll never see me do in my writings is bash the men I was married to because I went into sin and found them; therefore, I can't beat them up for being sinners. I'd sinned to get them, and then, I waited for them to get right with GOD. Howbeit, I share my testimony for the sake of keeping other women from falling into the same traps I had fallen into.

This book is for the single women who thinks my story is unrepeatable, and they'd never take what I took off a man. I used to say that as well, and anyone who knew me, knew I was serious. I was a confident woman who tossed men faster than a redneck tosses beer bottles. That's because

I was broken, and I saw men like lottery tickets; you'd lose many times before you actually won. But the truth is, there is one man out there that GOD will give permission to have you. Of course, if he goes off and marries a woman he chose for himself, GOD will bless another man with the opportunity to have your hand in marriage. There is no right way to sin, and if you sin your way into a relationship, sin will be the driving force that runs you out of it. Eve had Adam, Sarah birthed Isaac, and Ruth was blessed with Boaz, but what's your name and what do you have? There is one man who will reach across the hands of time to embrace, not just who you are today, but who you'll blossom into tomorrow. Every man can't be with you. What I learned from my marriages is that a man can love who you are when he meets you, but if you ever dare to become something better, you stand at danger of losing him. He fell in love with the old, sinful and rebellious you; but he could never love the new, righteous, and GOD-fearing woman that you'll grow to be someday. Only the man that GOD has custom-fitted for you will be able to cover you as you grow.

In this book, I am going to teach you what GOD taught me, as well as share parts of my testimony. My goal is to get you to stop making excuses and start waiting on GOD for your husband. As I mentioned before, I'm not the woman who did it right and can testify of a lengthy happy marriage; I am the woman who did it wrong twice, and can testify of the results of not doing it GOD'S way. I am blessed because GOD delivered me, not just from those marriages, but from that mindset I once had that led me into those marriages. Unfortunately, I run into many single women who are in that mindset and it's hard to show a woman the right way when she's convinced that the wrong way is gonna get her to what she wants a lot faster. The wrong way will get you the man you desire, but he won't be the man you need. Please understand that you are built to accompany your GOD-ordained husband, and HE is assigned to accompany you. Together, the two of you will be a powerful force against the enemy, and that's why the enemy works overtime to make sure you never link up with your GOD-ordained husband by sending you a well-wrapped devil.

When is Mr. Right Coming?

If you're like most single women, you want
to know when your turn will be to grace the
aisles at your church with Boaz on your arm.
You want to finally live that dream you've
had ever since you made Barbie marry Ken.
You've waited and waited, and you've
prayed without ceasing for your Mr. Right;
but where is he? Why is it that your friends
are getting married and having children, but
your Mr. Right is nowhere in sight? Has his
flight been delayed, or is he somewhere
married to Mrs. Wrong?

After ministering to so many single women,
here's what I've found out:

- **Most single women aren't single at
  all; they are still married to some
  man.** Let's face it. Anytime we
  engage in sexual activity with any
  man, that man becomes our

husband. Fornication doesn't mean that you're sleeping with a man you're not married to. Fornication means you've illegally wed a man through physical contact without your FATHER'S permission. It is to let a man uncover you physically before he covers you spiritually. Therefore, many women are still married to the men of their pasts. They haven't asked the LORD to divorce them from these men because they have yet to repent of those relationships. GOD won't send you a husband when you've already got one.

- **Many women in waiting have not forgiven a man or several men from their pasts.** Most of us have been hurt, and we can easily justify hating the men who've hurt us, but for what? Any man who has hurt you did so because he was likely not permitted by GOD to have you. You gave him you, and therefore, he did not know your value. To him, you were just another woman. If you don't forgive the men who've hurt you, GOD won't send you the right man because you'll make Mr. Right pay for the actions of Mr. Wrong and yourself.

- **Many women have not forgiven family members or friends.** A lot of women don't realize that unforgiveness of any sort is a hindrance. When someone wrongs us, what they are doing is bearing witness to the fact that they weren't supposed to be in our lives or that their season is up in our lives. Even for family members. Many believers continue associating with unrepentant sin-loving family members who continually rip the scabs off their hearts. They can never really heal because they are always in family drama.

- **Many single women refuse to close the doors on those relationships that have been binding them. These include family relationships as well as friendships.** Again, many single women have relationships that GOD has told them to walk away from long ago. Nevertheless, they hold onto these relationships because they think they need the people in them. Because of these open doors, GOD won't open the door for their husbands to find them, since in finding them, he's going to find all sorts of issues waiting to embrace him.

- **Many single women have items in their homes that bind them.** That diamond necklace your ex-boyfriend gave you may be beautiful, but it's also binding. Many women hold onto items from their past, and they wonder why they can't access the futures they want. You'd be amazed at how much power a little trinket has over you. Until you release everything that links you to the men of your past, you won't be able to hold onto any relationship, nor will GOD hand you the man of your future. Let go.

- **Many single women lust after themselves.** This one is probably not talked about a lot, but many single women masturbate. Masturbation is to have sexual contact with one's self. It's still a form of perversion because GOD did not create us to have intercourse with ourselves. If you ever want to know if a sexual act is a form of perversion, ask yourself this question: Can I get pregnant by engaging in it? If the answer is no, it's perversion. Everything GOD created was created to birth something.

Anytime you feel yourself strongly desiring sex to the point where masturbation starts to look inviting, you need to go on a fast and bind up anything unholy that's in, attached or trying to attach to you.

- **Many women are so full of voids that they are looking for a man to fill them.** GOD has a position in your life that HE is not willing to give up. HE is GOD, and HE wants to fill those voids in your life; nevertheless, many women refuse to let GOD fill their voids because they think these are areas that can only be filled by men. This is perverted thinking, and GOD knows that if a man was to fill that area, the woman would make an idol of him.

- **Many women don't have an intimate or consistent relationship with the LORD.** Many women are religious worshippers, and worshippers of

40

Sunday, but not worshippers of GOD. Because of this, many women worship GOD with their mouths, but their hearts are far from HIM. They call upon the LORD when they want or need something, but they don't call upon HIM when they are satisfied. In other words, many women attempt to use the LORD for their own selfish gain, lusts and needs; but they refuse to let HIM into their hearts.

- **Many single women are dating, not waiting.** You can't wait for Mr. Right while entertaining Mr. Wrong. Okay, so the world said we should date this man and that man until we find one worth marrying. If he happens to step outside our boundaries when married, we are to divorce him and wait and date some more. When you mature in the LORD, one thing you'll find is that you're not waiting on GOD

41

for your husband. You are waiting to be mature enough to be crowned as a wife. But many women lean to their own understandings, so they go out looking for their husbands on their own. When you are truly waiting on GOD for your husband, you'd give up dating and start waiting to be courted by "the" man GOD has for you. But when you are immature, you'll date any man who fits your understanding of what a husband should be.

- **Many single women have a problem with submission.** Okay, so this is where I step on the spirit of Jezebel's feet. You can't ask GOD for HIS son if you are not going to submit to him. GOD told us to submit to our husbands; that's HIS WORD. But when we hear the word "submit", many of us cringe at the thought because many of us don't truly understand what it means to submit.

42

To submit doesn't mean to be controlled; it means to trust the GOD who is leading your husband. Now, if you go out and meet a man who's not led by GOD, then you have a whole other issue on your hands.

- **Many single women want to be married for all the wrong reasons.** In my case, one of the reasons I wanted to be married was to have sex without sin being attached to it. I also wanted to fill some voids I had in my life; therefore, I wanted to marry for the wrong reasons. Ask yourself why you want to be married, and then answer yourself truthfully. What you'll oftentimes find is that you are seeking a man to fill a place in your heart that you have not yet opened up for GOD to enter.
- **Many single women are still babes in CHRIST; therefore, they are too young to marry.** When we are young

43

in the LORD, we always choose men who entertain our "right now" way of thinking. We don't understand that we're going to grow up in the LORD and what entertained us in 2013 won't necessarily entertain us in 2014. I am a living witness that when you feed on GOD'S WORD daily, HE will grow you up pretty quickly. If and when you become a mature, GOD-fearing Christian woman, you won't be so attracted to your immature, selfish and unbelieving man. Think about when you were four years old. If you were allowed to marry, who and what would you have chosen to marry? A clown likely, because he wears bright colors and he makes you laugh. We do the same thing when spiritually young. We choose clowns because they make us laugh and they wear flashy clothes. A babe in CHRIST will always be attracted to a decorated fool who's entertaining to her.

- **Many single women have a problem with men in general.** After having been hurt and hearing so many horror stories from women who've been hurt, we oftentimes forget that all men aren't the same. Many of us were taught that all men cheated, and we came to believe that a man had to be questioned, checked and corrected before he could be a decent man. This type of thinking is wrong, and it causes us to generalize men, rather than understand that there are many broken men out there who would happily get into a relationship with any woman who'd open up her life or her legs for them. And what can they do next? Men who walk in darkness often drag their women into the darkness. How you perceive men in general will affect

how you'll perceive your husband.
Change your perception, and you'll
get a clearer signal from the LORD.

- **Many single women are "looking"
  for their spouses.** The Bible said that
  "he" who finds a "wife" finds a good
  thing and obtains favor from the
  LORD. The issue is, we shouldn't be
  looking for our husbands. A wife is
  the crown to her husband. She is
  GOD'S way of saying that HE has
  approved the man to be a husband
  because HE knows the man will
  provide for her, love her and lead her
  in HIM. When a woman goes out
  searching for a man, she'll find many
  men who can't spiritually afford or
  cover her; therefore, they'll devalue
  and uncover her. A treasure never
  goes out looking for someone to
  reward itself to.
- **Many single women have iniquities
  hidden in their hearts.** Whatever we

have in us will flow from us. We are human beings who constantly have to get delivered from mindsets and beliefs. We are always introduced to new theories

- **Many single women are trying to keep themselves busy with the wrong things while waiting for Mr. Right.** From movies and music to associations, many single women try to occupy their time with people and things, rather than with GOD. As a result, they keep filling up on the wrong things and pushing Mr. Right further away. The right way to wait is to fill up on the WORD of GOD, so that GOD can enlarge you and declare you a blessing. If you're still looking to be blessed but refuse to be a blessing, you're not ready to be any man's crown just yet. Get the WORD in you, learn to cook more dishes, learn to do more things and tap into those gifts so that when Mr. Right comes along, you'll be a blessing to him, and he'll be a blessing to you.

- **Many waiting women want a man to bring something to the table, when they have nothing to offer him.** Many women today spend every dollar earned on adorning their flesh, but they rarely invest that money into building that ministry or that business GOD told them to build. In their minds, Mr. Right will come along and finance all of their dreams, and all they'd have to give him in return was their hand in marriage. Please understand that there are many women out there who'd happily give their hands in marriage to any man who wanted it; especially, a man anointed by GOD to be a husband. What makes you stand out from them? What do you have to offer? This doesn't mean you have to be rich, but you do need to be wealthy with wisdom, knowledge and understanding. You also need to be dependent on GOD, and not waiting for a man to come along for you to depend on. GOD won't send you a husband if you're going to be a yoke around his neck.

- **Many women have the wrong idea as to what it means to be a wife.** Ask the average woman what marriage is, and she'll quote a few movies she's watched. Many of us grew up with these wrong ideas about marriage, and we began to idolize the romantic aspect of marriage, but we didn't learn too much about the responsibilities of marriage. Because of this, many women continue to wait for their husbands. If he was released to them today and married them tomorrow, they'd be divorcing him by next week. Marriage is like a

49

job. You work hard at it, and it pays you in accordance with the work you've done. If you get too complacent in the marriage, you'll lose your benefits.

- **Many single women don't love themselves, and many don't even like themselves.** The problem here is that many women haven't even met their real selves yet. They've met who they've learned to be, and they've met different aspects of their personalities and strongholds, but they have yet to meet the flowers they truly are. Because of this, they devalue themselves and accept any man who seems to value them more than they value themselves. He becomes their validation, and GOD doesn't want this for us. You need to meet yourself before you introduce yourself to someone else. If you don't, that man will eventually walk

away from you when you blossom
into a beautiful rose because he
thought you'd grow up to be a cactus.
I started meeting myself while
married to Jay. The more I liked *me*,
the less I liked Jay.

- **Many single women do not love the
  LORD.** Anyone can go to church.
  Anyone can say they love the LORD,
  but our love for GOD is witnessed in
  our decisions. When we love GOD,
  we'll hate sin. But when our
  relationship with GOD is a religious
  and traditional ceremony that we
  think we must have on Sunday
  mornings, we are nothing more than
  sounding boards. To love GOD, you
  must get to know HIM better. If you
  put HIM last in your life, you'll meet
  all of the hurt, pain, betrayal and
  destruction that Satan has planned
  for you first. Once you put GOD as
  the head of your life, everything else

(health, sanity, prosperity) will follow. Love GOD first or you'll put sin ahead of HIM. If you put GOD first, HE will lead you into the blessings HE has provisioned for you.

- **Many single women compete with other women or see other women as threats.** Many women of the world have flawed thinking patterns. Oftentimes, many of these women see other women as threats; therefore, they compete with other women, ridicule other women, and attack other women. We have learned to expect this from the world, but this mentality has managed to bleed over into the church. Many believing women still have that competitive streak towards other women. One great way to see this is to add a bunch of believing women on Facebook, who have many of the same friends as you have. If you'll pay attention, you'll see that they'll like a man's post faster than they would another woman's post. Why is this? Many women want to be seen, validated and reassured by men; but other women are almost invisible to them.

- **Many single women don't want husbands to be husbands; they want life partners.** There is a Jezebel movement in the world, and it too has bled over into the church. Too many women are looking for men to follow them or partner up with them on their plans, but many don't understand that the Bible calls us help meets. Anytime the word "submission" or help meet is spoken of, a lot of believing women frown up and prepare to argue with the WORD. After all, we want to be equal with men, right? Who said we weren't equal? In GOD, we are equally loved, but GOD knows something about the build of a woman that most of us don't know. We were created from the rib of a man; therefore, we would have to be covered by a man. Adam was not created from another human being. He was created from GOD using the dust on the ground; therefore, he only had to answer to GOD. Being a wife doesn't mean you're a doormat; it only means that you've been granted with a blessed opportunity to walk with a husband who is led by GOD. Again, if you go out there and choose a man for yourself, he can't properly lead you, so he'll mislead you. And that's why so many women oppose the idea of being a wife, but treasure the idea of being a life pattern. Once you become a wife, you will be your husband's wife-partner, and you can relax and just be a lady.

Why Should I Wait?

Why should I wait for my husband to find me? I remember having that question many times, even though I'd never asked it aloud. Why did I have to wait when there were so many potential husbands walking about? In my mind, the role of a wife was to live with her husband, help him around the house, have sex with him, give him children, help him to raise those children, keep the house clean, cook the food, grow old with him, remain faithful to him and stay by his side until death. That was the distance that my understanding went, and I thought my understanding meant I'd be an awesome wife. I didn't consider that marriage is an institution created by GOD for GOD; therefore, I thought that going to church, praying often, and reading my Bible was what GOD expected from me. I was to be a woman of GOD but not a woman for GOD. When I did get married, I went above and beyond what I thought a wife was and a wife did. What I didn't know was that I was serving my own understanding and neglecting to serve GOD with my marriage. I thought marriage was for me, and my praise was for GOD. I wasn't the Proverbs 31 wife. I was just another married woman who worked hard to show the men who'd married me how appreciative I was of being called their wife.

Towards the end of my first marriage, GOD began to give me more wisdom, knowledge and understanding. I began to grow up in HIM, and I found myself hungering for a deeper relationship with HIM. When that marriage ended, my understanding continued to grow, and so did my hunger for the WORD. Once I met my second husband, I didn't realize that I was in the middle of a transition. I was growing up and maturing in the LORD. In the first year of marriage to my second husband, I'd outgrown the woman I once was when I met him. I was no longer willing to sin or lead a sinful life. I wanted more of GOD every day. During our first year of marriage, I began to regret marrying him. He was a sweet man in so many ways. He was gentle and passive towards others, but with me, he would be a rainbow of personalities that left me confused. The more I read my Bible and ministered to others, the more I'd realized that I'd made a big mistake.

What was happening with me? I was growing up, and as I grew up, I found that I wasn't fascinated by empty words anymore. I needed more. I hungered for more. I ached for more. And that's when the LORD began to minister to me, telling me what I was going through. I'd met a man while still young in the faith, and I was now growing up. I was no longer on milk. I was feeding on the meat of the WORD, and the man I was married to wasn't even born again yet. So what's the message behind this?

When you're young in the faith, you don't know you're young in the faith. Think of it the way you saw yourself when you were sixteen years old. You thought you were old enough to make your own decisions. You thought your parents' advice was outdated, and you thought you were ready to be an adult. As you got older, however, you realized just how naïve you were when you were sixteen. That's how it works in the faith. When you're a certain age spiritually, you think you're old enough to choose a man for yourself, or to choose what you would do to get that man. You thought your FATHER in Heaven just didn't understand, but HE would eventually come around once you introduced HIM to the man you'd chosen for yourself. You were so busy trying to outsmart your FATHER that

you forgot about your new father-in-law,
Satan.

Every day, many married women come to
the realization that they've married the
wrong men. They'd chosen their husbands
while in their youth, and now that they are
older in the LORD, they are no longer
attracted to the men at home. Their
husbands won't cover them in prayer. Their
husbands refuse to go to church with them,
and their husbands don't want to hang out
with their saved friends; they want to
continue hanging around their worldly
friends. Many married women find
themselves locked in an unhappy and
unfruitful marriage.

I remember being at church one Sunday,
when I was married the first time. I looked
over at a couple who were praising GOD
together. The husband had one hand
around his wife's waist and the other hand

raised in praise. I dropped my head in shame as I looked at the empty seat next to me. He didn't like coming to church with me, and over the years that we'd been married, he'd probably come with me to church four or five times. Every Sunday, I would see couples praising GOD together, and I wanted that so much. Every Sunday, I'd come home and tell him what I witnessed, hoping that he'd love me enough to give that to me. When I wanted furniture, he bought it for me. When I wanted a dog, he bought him for me. When he found out I loved makeup, he bought me a vanity table. There was no limit (money-wise) of what he'd spend on me, but the one thing he could not give me was free: a relationship with him in the LORD.

Nowadays, I meet women who ask me, "Can't I just marry my boyfriend now, and the two of us come to the LORD later?" My answer is always the same: "Yes, you could, but who's to say that he'll come to the LORD? As a matter of fact, he's going to expect you to remain the same sinful woman that he'd met and married. Once you begin to change, he'll begin to lose his attraction in you because he's not attracted to a godly woman. He wants a worldly woman. And let's say that he does decide to give his life to the LORD after you've married him. GOD still has to tear down the sinful foundation of your relationship with that man so HE can reestablish your relationship on the WORD. Most marriages do not survive this tearing down." Of course, I've seen less than a handful of women change their minds and wait on the LORD. But my joy is in seeing the few who do make that hard decision to walk away from their sinful relationships with their "boyfriends", and simply commit to waiting on the LORD.

But why should you wait? Here are a few

reasons.

- Everything in this earth starts off in seed time and ends in harvest. If you are sowing the seeds of righteousness, you will reap a righteous husband who will love, cover and provide for you for a lifetime. If you sow sin, you'll reap a sinner who will lust after you, expose you and take away from you for as long as you let him, or until he gets tired of you.

- GOD wants to grow you up first, so you'll learn to see marriage for what it really is. Too many women make marriage an idol and enter into the union expecting to serve it with their whole hearts. In this, they come out of the marriages with broken hearts and a destroyed idol. Always remember that in the olden days, when the people of GOD would have idols, GOD would command them to destroy those idols. If you make marriage an idol, it will be destroyed. Once GOD grows you up in HIM, you'll better understand what a marriage is, so you don't enter it expecting to serve it or for it to serve you.

- Your GOD-ordained husband may be getting dressed up by GOD for the union. In the natural, we dress the bride and groom before the wedding. We cover their bodies with beautiful apparel, and the bride is adorned in diamonds, pearls and makeup. GOD also dresses us for our big days, but HE adorns the inside of us. If you get with the right man in the wrong season, you will likely experience a marriage more broken and hurtful than you would have experienced with the wrong man in any season. Be patient, and let the LORD dress the two of you with wisdom, knowledge and understanding.

- GOD wants to fill those voids in the both of you. When you go into a marriage full of voids, you become dependent on the man in an unhealthy way. You become fearful, insecure and clingy, and these are all traits that scare men. Let GOD fill those voids first, and then HE'LL send Mr. Right your way.

- You must first release before you can receive. Many times, we have problems, secrets and fears that GOD wants to deliver us from before HE adorns a man's head with us. These problems, secrets and fears are potent enough to destroy ten marriages. We often hold onto the very things GOD is telling us to let go of.

- Let GOD give you the green light; otherwise, you'll crash into your own failed attempts to play GOD.

Waiting on GOD means that you trust HIM and that you will follow HIS lead. When you refuse to wait, you are saying that you don't trust HIM, and you will follow the lead of your flesh. The desires of the flesh lead to destruction; therefore, the flesh will never take you in the righteous direction. It will always lead you astray, and cause you to lean to your own understanding.

But you don't have to wait if you don't want to. You can go out there, choose the man you want, marry him and have children with him. But if you do that, prepare yourself for what is to come with him. You will never find a blessing in sin, and you will never find sin in a blessing.

Considering Your Options

We all want to know what our options are, right? After all, we live in a society where we are often afforded a choice in just about everything we want. So, it goes without saying that we often want to have multiple men to choose from. But that's not how it works.

In the world, the women gamble with their souls, lives and children by dating multiple men. Each woman wants to find a man who fits into her life like a perfectly fitted puzzle piece. Then again, there are those women who look for men who are visually appealing, and they try to change those men to get them to be a better fit for their lives. Nevertheless, nothing we do outside of GOD'S will is going to work.

So what options do we have? It's simple.
We can either wait on GOD or act like GOD,
but please know that if we choose the
latter, we will fail because we are not GOD.
When I was in the world, I remember
meeting women who had two men that
were interested in them. These women
tried to weigh out the pros and cons of each
man to decide which one they thought
would be the better fit for them. As typical
of worldly women, they chose the most
rebellious and unsettled one because he
represented the mysterious, whereas, the
more settled man was a wide-open book.
Years later, they'd be single with a few
children, and many times, these children
had different fathers. When I'd run into
them again, they'd be in a new relationship,
and they'd brag about the man they were
with. They'd ridicule the men they'd chosen
before, but they'd praise the one they were
currently with. A few years later, the good
guy would now be the bad guy, and another

great guy would be in his spot. What happened here? The woman did something GOD told her not to do. She leaned to her own understanding, so she found out again and again that she was not wise enough to choose a man for herself.

At any given moment, you'll have the attention of multiple men who think you'd look great on their arms or in their beds. Each man who pursues you represents something that is or was in you because we often attract what we are or what we were. If you marry a man who is attracted to the sin in you, he will lose interest in you once you get delivered from that sin, unless he too gets delivered. Of course, I said each man who "pursues" you, not each man who hits on you. Any man can hit on you simply because he wants to see what is in you or to boost his own self esteem.

In waiting for your husband, you do have

some things you need to make a decision on right now, so you won't make the wrong decision when it is imposed upon you later. It goes without saying that you should have already made up your mind that you will not have sex with a man until you're married.

Decide what you want in a husband. Sure, GOD has your Adam in store, but you can specify certain qualities that you'd like Adam to possess by the time he finds you. Please note that in requesting a lot, you may delay his arrival, because he has free will.

Decide what limitations a man has with you before he becomes your husband. For example, what hours of the night are off limits for phone calls? Will you hold hands or will touching be off limits? Will you kiss him or will you reserve that first kiss until your wedding day? It is better to make a list of what you want, and lay that list before the LORD. Some women who didn't wait will tell you that the list will keep you from getting married, but that's not entirely true. It'll keep you from marrying the wrong man. Anoint your list, pray over it and any man who doesn't want to give you the respect you're asking for is clearly not your husband.

Will you allow yourself to be alone with him, or will you proactively ensure that the two of you are never alone to keep temptation at bay?

Of course, I'd recommend that you are NEVER alone with a man who has not committed himself before GOD as your husband. You may be able to tell your ears that you won't fornicate, but it's hard to tell a burning flesh to cool off and behave itself.

What qualities do you not want in a husband?

This is just as important as deciding what you do want in a husband because it's easy to relax your standards when the man who's trying to win you looks like a winner.

How long are you willing to wait for a proposal?
You have to be honest with yourself and with the man who's courting you. If not, he may assume that it's okay to date you for eight years, whereas, you were hoping to get a proposal within a year.

How many kids and kids' mothers are you willing to accept?
The issue with settling is that we hope in our hearts that the men who approach us will have the qualities that we want in a husband, but we oftentimes don't say it aloud. When you make your requests known before the LORD, HE will honor your request. If you don't, you may end up with a man who's everything you don't want, and you'll have no one to blame for that but yourself. Remember, GOD said, "Ye have not because ye ask not."

If you're a mother, will you allow your husband to discipline your children?
Of course, the correct answer should be

yes. If you waited on GOD for him and GOD sends him, you can trust that HE has sent a man who will not only love you, but love your children as well. But when you choose a man for yourself, it is not wise to allow him to discipline your children because he's likely a temporary fixture.

One great thing to do is write out a list of scenarios that you'll likely encounter with your husband or husband-to-be. Ask yourself what you'd do in each scenario, and be honest with yourself. Be sure to be specific with the LORD as to what you want and don't want in a husband. That way, you'll be able to weed out Ishmael anytime he shows up. If you asked for a husband with two children or less, a stable job and someone who's easy on the eyes, but a man shows up with three kids, a seasonal job and a face only a mother could love, you know that GOD did not send him. GOD said HE would give you whatsoever you ask.

Satan often tries to negotiate with you, however. When he can't negotiate with you, he'll try bartering with you. He wants your soul, your anointing, your peace and your happiness; in exchange, he'll loan you one of his sons who fits some of your requirements. This is why it is very important to build a relationship with GOD; one where you know HIS voice, and the voice of a stranger, you will not follow.

How to Wait....Patiently

Have you ever wondered how a woman could sit there for years or decades waiting on her GOD-ordained husband? She remains poised in her faith, and she remains celibate for the entire wait. You sit back and marvel at her. Obviously, she was raised on a different foundation than you were, right?

One of the reasons many women have trouble waiting is because they aren't doing anything in the meantime. Many women live a life of repetitiveness, never seeking to go outside of what they understand. These women often expect a man to find them in their stagnation. Because of this, they often give up waiting and take the first man who they think they can mold into becoming Mr. Right. Show me a woman who's not operating in her purpose, and I'll show you a woman who doesn't know her worth. Such a woman will settle for any man who makes her feel valued. When waiting on GOD for a husband, you should always be busy doing the will of GOD so your husband will find you in the LORD. Anytime a woman doesn't busy herself with the purpose GOD has placed in her, she'll become a distraction to any man who comes into her life.

As a business owner, I rarely have time to have fruitless conversations with people. Every conversation I have has to be fulfilling. Either I have to be blessed or I need to be a blessing. One of the things that happened to me over the years was that I'd meet women, and we'd talk and eventually become friends. I was married, and many of them were not. At that time, I didn't understand that GOD had placed many of them in my life for a season, but once that season was up, they would be released from my life. I was a wife and business owner; therefore, I didn't have a whole lot of time for pointless chit chat. I've lost a few friends because I could not and would not speak with them every day for several hours a day. What I would do was to try to push them into operating in their purposes, and they'd promise to get started in their businesses and ministries. Nevertheless, I'd get another call later that evening, and then the next day and they'd talk about their day. I'd start pushing them again, but each push began to become agitating to them because they did not want to get into purpose; they wanted to entertain their boredom. Each of these women were allegedly waiting on GOD for their husbands. After a while, I started telling them every day that I was busy. It didn't take long before they became upset with me, and they distanced themselves from me...thank GOD.

What's the point of this story? It's obvious. These were women who weren't doing anything; therefore, they became a burden to me....a woman who was just their friend. Can you imagine how much of a burden they'd be to a man? The point is that if you are not adding anything to that man, you'll only take away from him.

The only way you can wait patiently for your husband is by getting busy in purpose. A woman who's busy doing what GOD told her to do, or created her to do, won't have too much time to feel lonely. She'll be too busy to pity herself or envy everyone else who's getting married. What you have to do is identify the purpose in you, and get active in it. What are you passionate about? What would you love to do? Who would you love to help? Just getting out and volunteering at some shelters or nursing homes would do you a world of good. Just building and working that business GOD gave you would keep your mind occupied. Just getting out there and ministering to others will help you to minister to yourself. You have to add on to who you are, and not expect a man to come along and add value to you. Consider the example I gave of my old friends. Because they weren't busy, they wanted to take up too much of my time. The only way I could have a friendship with them was if I'd stopped operating in my purpose to become their phone buddies.

And just because you're in ministry doesn't mean you're fully in purpose. That's the trap so many believing women fall into. What you are doing now may just be a layer of who you are, but it may not be the full picture. You have to continue to build upon what GOD gave you, and GOD will continue to build you up. The seasons are like vehicles driven by impatient taxi drivers. When they come around, you'd better be ready, or you'll get left behind.

Here a few suggestions that should help you

along your wait.

- Buy a notebook or journal and list the gifts and talents you have.
- In that notebook, create a page for each gift or talent, and list what you are going to do with it.
- Open a Word document on your computer and create a business plan or ministry plan.
- In a separate document, create a schedule for yourself. Be sure to follow that schedule every day until it becomes second nature to you.
- List self-imposed penalties that you will place upon yourself for those days when you did not operate in your purpose. Make sure these penalties are big enough to get your own attention.
- Get an accountability partner, if you know someone who's anointed and purposeful.
- At least once a week, get out and

help someone somewhere. You can go to a shelter, orphanage, nursing home, jail or just around your city.

- Put money to the side for your business and/or ministry. Create a savings account or a checking account, and refuse to touch that money unless it's going towards what it was intended to go towards.
- If you need to, get a makeover. Sometimes, something as simple as a change of appearance is motivating enough to get you started.
- Surround yourself with busy women who are all operating in their purpose, and distance yourself from slothful people who aren't doing anything but talking. Believe it or not, a woman who's not doing anything will do much to keep you from doing anything.
- Ask GOD to reveal your gifts and cause you to walk in them. Commit

to being faithful with your gifts and to glorifying HIM only with those gifts. A woman who takes a talent and glorifies herself is a magnet for devil-filled men who want to use her talents to glorify themselves.

There are many things you can do to wait on your husband. If you do these things for the glory of GOD and to bless HIS people, you will:

- Cause GOD to move in favor of you.
- Cause the blessings of GOD to pursue and overtake you suddenly.
- Be found by your husband faster than most women.
- Discover who you are in the LORD.
- Discover what you can do in the LORD.
- Cause the enemy to flee from you.
- Show GOD that you are faithful enough to HIM; therefore, you'll be faithful to the husband HE sends you.

In the Meantime

What can you do while you are waiting on Mr. Right? Of course, in the chapter above, we discussed how to wait patiently, but are there any recreational things you could do while you wait? I'll answer that with a testimony.

When I was married to Jay, I found myself feeling starved. I felt starved of love, attention, affection and everything a woman craves from her husband. I asked him to at least take me out to eat once a week, and he agreed.
Our favorite spot was Red Lobster, and I treasured those dates. Every week, I would look forward to Saturday because I knew we'd be sitting in Red Lobster as a couple. At home, Jay was distant, but when we went out to eat, there was nothing else for

him to do but talk with me. I didn't care what we talked about. He was my husband and I wanted him to be as interested in me as I was in him.

When Jay realized how important these dates were to me, he began to use them as a weapon whenever I offended him.

One day, we were supposed to go out to eat at my favorite spot: Applebees. I'd gotten dressed and was sitting on the couch waiting on Jay, who was standing a few feet away in the kitchen. I don't remember what we got into an argument about, but I remember how easy it was for Jay to cancel our date. He said to me that the date was canceled and if I wanted to eat out, I would do so alone. I was upset by this because I'd been looking forward to that date all week, and I'd went out of my way to look beautiful for him. Jay then went into the freezer and took some food out. He told me that he was cooking himself something to eat, and I could eat it if I wanted, but we weren't going out. I remember feeling hurt, but then, a peace came over me. The LORD laid it upon my heart to take myself out. I was dressed, I felt beautiful, and I wanted to go out, so I did.

During the drive to Applebees, I began to pray and ask GOD to give me peace and let me enjoy myself. I didn't want to look at other couples and pity myself. I didn't want to not enjoy my meal because there was no one sitting across from me. I didn't want to waste money on food if I wasn't going to eat it.
When I finally arrived, I went into the restaurant feeling great. The hostess led me to my booth, and I opened up my IPAD. I noticed that Applebees also had a new gadget on their table where I could play games. I sat there and I felt wonderful; truly wonderful. I felt empowered, loved and appreciated by GOD. I could feel my

FATHER'S presence with me. I looked at
other women coming in and dining with
their beaus, and it didn't hurt me. Instead, I
thought to myself, *how many women are in
here with their Ishmaels?* I knew that most
of the women in that restaurant were there
with a man GOD hadn't ordained for them.
I had a huge appetite that day. I even
ordered dessert. I didn't rush to leave the
restaurant either. Instead, I sat there and
relished in every moment. From that day
forward, anytime Jay would back out of our
dates to punish me, I'd get up and go with
the LORD.

After Jay and I broke up, I had no problem
dining alone. One day, I went to Olive
Garden, and as I was sitting in my booth, I
noticed a father and daughter in a booth
ahead of me. The scene was so beautiful to
me. The father appeared to be in his mid-
fifties, and the daughter appeared to be a
teenager about seventeen years old. He

may have been her grandfather, but I think
he was her father. Anyhow, he was so
attentive to her, even though she seemed to
be a little distracted by everything going on
around her. That's how I envisioned that I
was with my FATHER. HE was sitting there
with me, very attentive of me, but I was
distracted by so many things going on in my
life. Nevertheless, he loved and still loves
me.

My advice is obvious. Get out and court the
LORD. Go and eat out with no one sitting
with you, but GOD. Invite GOD out with you
everywhere you go. Go shopping with HIM.
Go to the park with HIM. Spend time alone
at home with HIM. Too many women
occupy their time with people, and they
become dependent on a human presence,
and this can be crippling to the way we
think.

About two years before my marriage ended

with Jay, GOD started teaching me how to be alone. I'd never learned to be alone before, but here I was in a state far away from my family. I had no friends in that state, so I absolutely was physically alone, but GOD was with me. Jay and I used to walk together every day to exercise, but there were times when he'd work late, so I had to walk by myself. At first, this was excruciating to me because I was so accustomed to having him with me. Then, he'd announce he'd be going out of town for a week or more, and I would find myself all alone once again. I would try to call my friends when I went for my walks, but what I found was that they never seemed to answer their phones. But when I arrived home, they would return my calls. It didn't take long for me to realize that GOD wanted to walk with me. HE wanted to speak with me, and HE wanted to teach me that I only needed HIM.

After a while, I began to enjoy those walks.

When I became a single woman, I enjoyed those walks all the more.

What should you do while you wait for Mr. Right? Spend time with your FATHER. Anytime you associate a human being with an area of your life, you have just found a void in your life. That's a place you need to fill with GOD, not a person. I hear a lot of women say they couldn't dine alone; therefore, they call their friends and ask them to dine with them. In doing so, the woman never gives herself the time to get to know herself better. Believe it or not, the husband you choose for yourself or the husband GOD sends you is going to mold you. You won't realize you've been molded if you never take time out for yourself and the LORD. If you spend too much time with people, you'll easily forget about your own likes and desires, and you'll focus too much of your energy trying to be what a man likes and desires. GOD specifically created you for one husband, and that husband will only lead you in the LORD, helping you to become a better woman. Any other man will lead you to himself, helping you to become a better woman for him, but not the LORD.

In the meantime, I challenge you to interview ten women. Talk with three who are happily married to their GOD-ordained husbands, talk with three who are married to Ishmaels, talk with two who are celibate and waiting on GOD for their husbands, and talk with two divorced women. Ask them some pointed questions.

Ask the women in relationships, and the divorced women, the following questions:

- Did you wait on GOD for your husband?
- Did you fornicate to get him?
- What were some of the challenges you faced while waiting for him?
- What were some of the challenges

you faced while with him?
- What lessons did you learn from your experiences with men?
- What advice would you give a single, saved woman?

Ask the women who are saved and celibate the following questions:
- Why did you choose a life of celibacy?
- How many men have been warded off by your choice to remain celibate?
- Was celibacy a challenge for you?
- What lessons did you learn from your experiences with men?
- What lessons have you learned from being celibate?
- What advice would you give a single, saved woman?

What you'll find is that the women who chose to wait on GOD came out with some men worth waiting for. The women who sinned their way to the altar ended up marrying blazing sinners who fed the sin in them but starved them of the WORD. Also, ask the celibate women how many men have run away from them just because they chose to be obedient to GOD? The purpose of the wait is to get the devil and his children to flee from you, but women who don't wait, end up heading to the altar twice: One time for marriage, and another time to repent of that marriage.

In the meantime, stay busy in the LORD. As I mentioned earlier, a woman who does not operate in her purpose is oftentimes clingy, demanding and draining. Imagine how much of a snare such a woman would be if she were given full-time access to a man. Don't be her.

She Got Married...You Didn't

One of the things I have often heard single women say is how hard it is to watch another woman get married, especially if that woman sinned her way in. I was still married to Jay when I first started hearing this, so I had a worthy answer waiting for them. I was once that woman who was being taken to an altar...or at least, a courthouse. Many women looked upon me in awe as I brandished my sin before them. For a while, I made sin look good, and that's why I had to come back out of it and tell the women what it truly looks like without the mask.

You see your friend, family member or co-worker running around showing off her new engagement ring. You know she's been shacking with her guy for quite some time.

She's always driving a nice car, her hair is always sharp, and her clothes are always trendy. She marries her beau, and every time you see her, it seems as if she always has good news. Now, her and her new husband are buying a new house in a great area. She's always smiling, and sin seems to be working for her. Then comes the news that she's pregnant....again. You look in awe and think to yourself that you've been trying to do things the right way, only to find yourself still alone years later.

If You Wait on GOD

Finally, Mr. GOD-ordained finds you, and your relationship with him grows stronger by the day. It turns out that he doesn't believe in fornicating or kissing before marriage either. He's thrilled to see a woman who loves the LORD as much as you do. He knows who you are. You are his crown, and he's finally been favored by GOD to have you. One day, he proposes, and you accept. Not long after that, the two of you are married with a baby on the way. Life is great, and you praise the LORD with your husband daily.

One day, you hear about that co-worker who once made sin look inviting. It turns out that her husband had an adulterous affair and left her to be with another woman. Her house is in foreclosure, and now her hair and clothes are unkempt. When you see her driving down the highway, she's no longer driving that fancy car. Now, the lesson hits you. Satan made sin look good through her to cause other women to fall into his snare. He wanted to cause you and others like you to stumble. She was just a template for sin. Cigarette ads make cigarettes look great, but nicotine is deadly to the human body, and so is sin. She was nothing more than a billboard for Satan, but once he'd had his fun with her, he'd stripped her of the very glory you once stood in awe of. I was her. I had the appearance of happiness, and I had all the material things I wanted, but I didn't have joy. In my first marriage, I ended up with the big house and all of the beautiful furniture, but I was tormented by the things going on in that marriage. Guess what? That marriage ended. In the second marriage, I traveled to so many countries and had so many material things, but I didn't have joy, peace or security. Guess what? That marriage ended. In marrying the wrong man, you sacrifice the valuable things that every woman needs, such as love, joy, peace and security, for the sake of appearing to be happy. Sure, you have a man at home, but you'll still find yourself lonely and waiting for your husband to show up. Even though you're married to that man you chose, he's present in body, but his mind is elsewhere. So you wait on him to come around or for GOD to remove him from your life. Either way...you have to wait on GOD.

When you see a woman walking with a man, don't envy her. Oftentimes, if you knew what was going on in her life, you'd pity her. Now, this isn't to say that you should find pleasure in another woman's pain. This is to say that you should understand that a smile doesn't always equate to happiness, and a frown doesn't always equate to misery. When a woman is found by her GOD-ordained husband, you should be happy because GOD is being glorified. At the same time, it is reassuring to see GOD blessing someone else for their faithfulness, because it lets you know that you're up next for a promotion if you stay in HIS will.

Anytime I see a couple together, I don't think of who they are to one another either way. It's not my business. He's likely not her GOD-ordained husband, and I know their relationship will probably end within ten years or less. I'm not caught up in appearances anymore because I was once the woman who appeared to have it all, but behind closed doors, I was miserable. I was always looking for a happy day because my life was an unpredictable mess.

Learn to celebrate other women, and at the same time, you should learn to appreciate the testimonies you have. Each failed relationship should have served as a lesson to you. Don't walk around looking at other folks and their relationships. Focus on your relationship with the LORD, and HE will add the husband to you that HE knows will be everything you want and need, plus more. Women who tend to focus on the relationships of others often find themselves entering relationships with the wrong men. It's similar to something I once said to a little girl who was in a dance group. I knew she was a great dancer, and she was a confident dancer around the people she knew. She'd messed up a dance routine because she was watching another girl who was dancing beside her. I told her that she needed to make her own mistakes and to never watch another dancer; it'll only throw her off beat. That lesson applies to every woman who wants to live a life that's pleasing to GOD. If you want to stay in tune with GOD, don't watch the woman beside you. If you do, you'll mess up whenever she messes up. GOD has a unique story for you to tell one day, but Satan has also designed a script that he'd like you to read from. Your obedience or lack thereof will determine which role you get.

50 Obvious Ishmaels to Avoid

As discussed earlier, there is only one man who GOD has ordained to marry you. One of the hardest things to do is part through the brown, white, beige and red sea of idiots to be found by the right one. Of course, in being found, you don't have to try to discern who's who in your life. You simply need to obey GOD, and if the man who's pursuing you was not sent by GOD, your obedience to GOD will send him running back into the devil's arms for safety.

Some men are obviously Ishmaels. Sadly enough, many of these men get past discernment and find themselves standing at the altar (or courthouse) with the women of their dreams; women whose lives are about to become a reoccurring nightmare.

In this section, you are going to recognize many of the Ishmael traits I'll mention. You will laugh and may even recognize your guy in here, but the right thing to do is take it seriously, and take it before the LORD. And let me say this before you proceed: this section can be entertaining, educating or offensive. If you happen to recognize certain characteristics as traits your spouse or beau has, don't automatically assume that he's an Ishmael. Some men may be saved, sanctified and filled with the HOLY GHOST, but still need to be delivered from wrongful thinking.

Additionally, a lot of these characters you'll find are worldly; therefore, you probably wouldn't get with them anyway. As with everything, be sure to lay your guy's name at the altar of GOD before proceeding into a relationship with him.

The Ex-Terminator

This guy has one woman he's crazy about,

and he uses other women to make her jealous. Sometimes, he's not even crazy about the woman. Sometimes, he uses other women in an attempt to control the woman he has.

The Rescuer
This guy is a hopeless romantic. He's often strong, good-looking and romantic. He often rescues women from bad relationships or recent break-ups. He fuels his self-esteem by rescuing these women, but once they get too comfortable with him, he suddenly leaves them without a formal goodbye. His issue is that he's actually looking to be rescued from the low self-worth he feels. He knows that he's good-looking, and he loves women who are needy. He can provide things for them that the previous guy could not provide, but he's usually one pretty messed up guy if you get past his demons.

The Guy Who Needs Rescuing

He's in a bad relationship, and he's got plenty of stories to tell you. In his stories, he comes off as the catch of a lifetime, while his girlfriend or wife is portrayed as a monstrous creature who speaks in the tongues of demons. If you fall for his words, he'll cause you to dislike (or even hate) his significant or insignificant other. If he gets you full-time, you will eventually become the monster at home that he tells other women about. Make no mistake about it. He's a good actor, but he's a lost cause.

The Chameleon

He changes his personality to fit yours temporarily. If you are an obvious Christian woman, he claims that he's always wanted a "church" girl because she may be able to help him change. He's a liar, and his forked tongue will dance around in a woman's ear until she gives him a chance to show off his real colors. If you get with this guy, he will come to church with you a few times. He may even approach the altar during altar call, but he'll eventually drag you away from the church. His method is to get you to love him to the point where you would do anything to keep him. It is then that he'll begin to pull you away from the LORD.

Mr. Controlling

This guy is three miles to the left of crazy, and he doesn't know it. He's always correcting his woman, and you can never seem to be right about anything. He's often emotionally and verbally abusive. Eventually, he begins to physically attack the woman he's been controlling. This is a very dangerous man, and any woman who allows him to control her, puts herself in danger. Power is addictive, and any man who touches it becomes ensnared by it. Many men who killed the women in their lives were of this "species" of men, and many of the women they'd killed once allowed these men to control them. When they attempted to take back control over their own lives, they were met with a man who did not know how to release that power. It's not them he was obsessed with; it was the power he had over them. If you'll notice, he rarely (if ever) stalked the women who did not allow him to control them. He simply left them. But the women who were controlled by him were beaten, stalked, harassed, and many of them were killed.

Mr. Most Likely to Kill Someone

This character is definitely similar to the Controller, but he only seeks women that he can intimidate. He is addicted to fear and power. He only dates and marries women who have low self-esteem and are easily intimidated.

The Faller

This guy is very charming, and he falls in love very easily; therefore, many women fall

in love with him. That's why he's a faller.
He is usually the one who brings the
greatest heartbreak to a woman because he
fills her up with hope and lies, and he
showers her with affection. He's usually
smitten within the first week or less. The
issue with him is that he truly falls in love,
but he will fall out of love just as fast as he
fell in love. The Faller has to be kept high
on love and does not fare well in normal
relationships. He has to be on cloud nine or
he'll find someone else to take him there.
He'll genuinely fall in love with the new
woman, and then every woman after her.
He also marries women pretty easily,
proposing to some women within days or
weeks of meeting them. A Faller often plays
music in the background or whenever he is
in your presence because he's led by the
lyrics and turned on by the idea of living
those lyrics. That's why he's a faller.

Height Seeker

This guy belongs to the Faller class. He loves the highs of new relationships, but once that new car smell wears off, he's off in search of a new woman. Unlike the Faller, however, he doesn't stay in relationships long. He's only there a few months, and once things begin to level off, he starts shopping for a new woman to climb. A Height Seeker also likes to do daring things in an attempt to add a spark to the relationship.

Depth Seeker
He loves to take his woman to the lowest of lows for the sake of making up. He's perverted in this thinking and in every way. A Depth Seeker will seek to start an argument about anything, and he'll take a small issue and turn it into a major issue. The problem is, the greater the fight, the more he gets turned on. He's a broken soul who loves the thrill of a good fight, and he is oftentimes physically abusive as well.

The Charmer
He loves to find women who are not accustomed to having nice things, and then he buys them the world. He usually has a good job or is fairly wealthy. He often trolls the poorest areas of town in his Lexus, BMW or Mercedes looking for women. Once he finds one he wants to prey on, he will wine and dine her. He pays her bills, and he may even buy her a car. Once she gets too comfortable with him, however, he loses interest and looks for another project to rescue. When he settles down, it is never with a woman from a bad area. He often settles with successful women; nevertheless, he continues to patrol the poor areas in search of someone to rescue. In his own twisted way, he's giving back to society.

The Whiner
This guy complains about everything,

including the weather. Even though his mother spoiled him, he is not too close to her. Sometimes, he's nice and loving. Other times, he'd leave you to wonder whether or not he is going through P.M.S.

Momma's Boy

A Momma's Boy can't do anything without his mother's approval. Most of his clothes were bought by his mother, and she continues to spoil him rotten. He is likely very feminine in nature, and is often found gossiping alongside a group of women. He's oftentimes a great cook.

The Sexual Pervert

This twisted character relates everything in life to sex. You can lead him one way in a conversation, but he'll always bring the conversation back to sex. The Sexual Pervert often tests women in the beginning of the relationship by asking questions about anything sexual. If rebuked, he'll likely go away. The Sexual Pervert often frequents porn sites and can be found at a mall near you, trolling for women.

Mr. Metrosexual

He often makes a great conversationalist and friend, but even though he says he's straight, his mannerisms show otherwise. He's often great at cooking, decorating or applying makeup on a woman. He may be straight, however, so don't brush him off completely. Take his name before the LORD, lay it at the altar and leave it there until you get a clear answer from GOD about him. Some metrosexuals were just raised by women and picked up a lot of feminine ways.

The Clothes Hanger

He's in the closet, but when outside, he loudly and adamantly protests against homosexuals. Oftentimes, he is bisexual or gay, and he uses his projected hatred as a cover to camouflage the demons within him. Sure, we all know that homosexuality is wrong, but the Clothes Hanger will make it his personal mission to confront every gay man he sees. He'll often hold a conversation for hours on end as to why he hates gays, but he's usually exposed when one of his lovers come forth or he's caught in the act.

The Thug
What rapper or hip hop artist is he channeling today? His personality will always depend on who's hot in the hip hop industry, so if you want a fair shot at him, you'd better stay abreast of today's hip hop fad. He belongs to the Follower's class, and he's often very rebellious. He pretends to be strong, but he has security around him at all times, and that security is: a pit-bull (or whatever dog his favorite rapper has), a gun and a few friends. His car and what little money he has often comes first, his friends

are second, and you'd better "get in where you fit in."

Mr. Bragger

He's always talking about the good he's done for people. In his words, he has helped many. If you pay attention to his stories, you'll notice that he always seems to be at the right place at the right time. He's also very condescending towards the people in his story who did not help out the people who needed help. Marry him, and you'll find out that he's not only a compulsive liar, but he needs psychological help.

The Available Ex

This guy is clearly still in love with his ex-girlfriend or ex-wife. He speaks about her all the time, and he's oftentimes still in contact with her. Throughout all of her failed relationships, he is there to offer her some advice. He says that they are just friends, but the truth is, he's still in a relationship with her...she just doesn't know it. He even goes to her house to help her put furniture together and he never forgets her birthday...ever. But he will forget yours.

Mr. Falsely Accused

He has many arguments with his mother and siblings. According to him, he's the black sheep of the family. Trouble follows him, but he claims that he's innocent and being falsely accused. Everything is a setup; even when he got arrested...it was all a misunderstanding or a setup.

The Car's Wife

He takes really good care of his car, often washing it daily. He doesn't like fingerprints on his car, and will often park at the far end of a parking lot to make sure his car doesn't get a scratch on it. If a scratch is found, he'll overreact. When women get into a relationship with him, they usually threaten to do damage to his car when provoked. Many of his exes have done things to his car or cars because they knew he was his car's wife.

Mr. Mysterious

Oh, how we loved him on the big screen. Every time we saw a movie where the actor was handsome and mysterious, we drooled and fantasized about being the leading lady in the movie. But the actual Mr. Mysterious is often full of secrets, very perverse and sometimes criminally insane. When you see this character with his friends, he's often the shy, cute guy. If a woman chooses him over his friends, they often stand by in awe because they know something about him that most of the women who approach him don't know. Men tend to nickname their friends according to what they know about them. It is always better to ask his friends for his nickname, and if it has any "insane" notes to it, let Mr. Mysterious remain a mystery.

Mr. Coward

Yes, we are supposed to turn the other cheek when slapped, but this guy is just everyone's punching bag. Mr. Coward often doesn't know how to say "no" to people on the outside, but he has no problem saying "no" to you (the woman at home). When this character has been intimidated and humiliated yet again, he often comes home and takes it out on his Mrs. This helps him to feel like a man again. He's oftentimes very abusive and can be quite dangerous. He will usually harass an ex until one of her male relatives threatens him.

The Goalless Horseman

This man's plans include retiring from a low-paying, dead-end job that he's had for decades, having a few kids, and frequenting his family's houses for snacks, barbeques and football games. With Goalless, you pretty much know what you're getting, and that is a boring life where the only thing you can watch grow is his stomach.

The Dreamer
This character has many ideas about businesses he wants to start, or he often says he's going to return to school. He's similar to Mr. Goalless, only he does have a vision for something better. The problem is, he has absolutely no drive to do anything; therefore, he's got more words than he has plans. He often sees new friendships as opportunities because he's always hoping that success will fall from behind one of his ears. For example, if he meets or links up with a guy who has a decent paying job, he'll likely ask the guy to help him get on with that company. If the guy agrees to do so, Mr. Dreamer will often come home and tell you the good news. If hired, however, he's likely to work a few weeks or a few months before quitting because he is not

looking for actual work. He wants easy pay with little to no effort.

The Punk Rocker

This man is full of tattoos, piercings and other weird obstructions to his body. His hair has likely seen more hair colors and hairdos than it can handle. This guy is usually on drugs and always looking to get high. His unlucky lady in love is oftentimes a youthful junkie whose beauty hasn't yet succumbed to her drug use.

Mr. All About His Friends

This character loves hanging out with his friends, and feels a need to prove himself as abnormally loyal to them. He is usually surrounded by a variety of personalities, most of which are womanizers and users. He will easily break up with any woman who doesn't like his friends, humiliates him in front of his friends or who isn't liked by his friends. Oftentimes, this character has that one decent friend who tries to tell him to stop being so loyal to a bunch of guys who aren't loyal to him; nevertheless, he remains poised in his ignorance. He's often taken advantage of by his friends once they realize he's constantly paying for his membership to the group by breaking up with women, making their enemies his enemies and doing whatever they want for the sake of being accepted.

The Apologizer

The Apologizer has a weird obsession with offending his lovers, only for him to apologize to them. Closely related to the Height Seeker class, the Apologizer thrives on the ups and downs of relationship drama. He has no problem admitting that he was wrong, but he does have a problem doing what's right.

The Self-Erected Idol

This fellow enjoys attention and anyone

who idolizes him. He seeks to project himself in a hero-like way, and he's always helping others for the sake of getting compliments. He will always go and help his family members or friends when they need a helping hand, but it's not because he loves them. It's often because he's trying to gain and maintain the respect and worship of others. This character will not remain in relationships where he's not worshipped.

The False Prophet
He tells you that GOD said you were his wife, and he's also told several women that in the past. This character is extremely wicked and portrays himself as a religious man. He preys upon women who are babes in CHRIST, not born again or women who are on the rebound. He often complains about others in church leadership and can't hide his desire to ascend up the ranks in the church. This dark character will often leave a church if he's not immediately given a

place of power within that church or if he's not elevated as fast as he wants to be. Warning: This character often has a warlock and a python spirit.

The Hypocritical Pervert
He openly teaches against fornication, but has a CD collection that boasts of every song people love to fornicate to. He will portray himself as a righteous man, but any woman who speaks with him for a week or more will soon discover how perverted he really is. This character will often slyly mention sex or a sexual act to see how far he can go with the woman on the other line. If not rebuked, his devils show themselves in full array.

The Devil's Advocate
A religiously twisted character, this man hates holiness and anyone who displays holiness. He will often stand up for sin and sinners but is rarely found standing up for

righteousness. This character surrounds himself with sinners and justifies this behavior by stating that JESUS sat with tax collectors and sinners. The issue with him is, he is a sinner, but somehow he was given a title, rank and responsibilities; therefore, he strives to find a perfect bridge between sin and righteousness. Also referred to as the Devil's lawyer, he will help others to cover their sin, and go up against the ranks of people who come against sin. He is likely to never deal with you unless you get caught up in a scandal and need demonic representation.

Ahab

Ahab always needs a Jezebel, so men like this are often attracted to aggressive, independent and demonically led women. They don't fare well in relationships with normal women and will often find a Jezebel to control them, whether she be in his family or in his church. This character will often take the woman he's with through a whole lot of hurt, but to others on the outside, he appears to be passive, harmless and sweet. In truth, he's a passive-aggressive devil who flourishes in the presence of openly aggressive women and men. Ahabs are usually fearful of others, and will often whine to the Jezebel they've handed their testicles to about the events of each day. Anytime someone offends or scares an Ahab, he runs and tells Jezebel because he trusts in her leadership and not his own.

The Educated Foosball
This guy has read one too many books, and he's now a Mr. Know-It-All...at least, in his own world. It's pretty difficult to have a conversation with this character because he knows (or thinks he knows) the history behind just about everything. He does not like to be corrected but loves a good debate. I called him a Foosball because he's

tossed to and fro with every wind of doctrine. He's read the entire Bible, the Qur'an, the Torah and every religious document under the sun. He isn't really sure if he believes totally in the LORD JESUS CHRIST, but often refers to HIM as a mere man. He can talk for hours, often talking himself to sleep. This character is sometimes bordering Agnostic, is fully Agnostic or Atheist. The religious version of this man often goes from one religion to the next every time he feels he's been "enlightened." He often sees Christianity as a form of mental bondage.

Mr. Almost There

He seems to always be down on his luck, but things are beginning to look up for him. Every time you find him, his car will reportedly be in the shop, he'll have an interview scheduled at a promising job, and he'll have other opportunities in the making. Amazingly enough, he never seems to arrive at his destination.

The Woman Hater

This poor guy has been done wrong by just about every woman he's had, starting with his mother. He always has horror stories to tell about his exes, but will speak highly of you because you are his current interest. Once you become an ex, he'll rant and rave about how awful you were as well.

Mr. Borrows

This man borrows everything! He borrowed the car he picked you up in for your date, he borrowed the outfit he's wearing, and he needs to borrow money from you once the date is finished. It seems that he has forgotten to bring his wallet. This guy is looking for a woman to take care of him and is not interested in being the provider for a family. He will try to get as much as he can out of a woman because he knows he's living on borrowed time with her. Every woman who dates him ends up tossing him because of his laziness and his lack of ambition.

Mr. Adrenaline

This guy loves fast cars and he loves to tempt death. He lives life on the edge and often tempts GOD with his search for a new high. He doesn't stay in relationships long unless he finds a woman who's just as daring as he is.

Mr. Self

Mr. Self is all about himself at all times. Everything you do or say has to be all about him; otherwise, he'll start an argument. Arguments, to him, are opportunities for him to show himself as the victim or the better one. When eating out, he prefers to dine at his favorite restaurants. Any and everything he does, and expects you to do, is all about him. He's similar to the Self-Erected Idol, but he doesn't always require verbal worship or compliments. He just needs to see you working hard to make him happy.

Mr. Fetish
Of course, this guy belongs to the Sexual Pervert class. He seems to have fetishes with certain body parts or material things. He may be sexually sadistic and is "turned on" by strange things like certain noises or acts that a normal man wouldn't think twice about.

Mr. Fighter
This guy is a bad boy and a good fighter, but fighting doesn't pay the bills. He's often found unemployed and hanging around a bunch of guys who see him as nothing more than their pit-bull.

Mr. Referee
This gentleman is a womanizer who loves to put women up against one another. Often

playing the victim role, Mr. Referee often has a wife or a woman he lives with, but he'll have multiple affairs and tell his mistresses all types of awful lies about the woman who's serving him full-time. His desire is to see the women fighting over him because this boosts his often low self-esteem.

Clyde

Clyde is a criminal who has a position open for a Bonnie. He often finds women who have low self-esteem, and he presents himself to them as a strong, rebellious character who the world is against. In his mind, he will be wealthy one day; he just has to find the perfect con. He's usually a faithful guy when he finds a woman who's willing to be his Bonnie, but make no mistake about this guy. Once caught, he'll often point the fingers at the woman who foolishly served him.

Satan's Biggest Fan

This character is often into horror movies or action films, and he often sides with the villain. He sees himself as a villain, and the world as being against him. This man often borders schizophrenia and will do the worst things to any woman who opens her heart to him.

The Weird Guy

This man can be nice unless you mess with his comic book collection. He's often out of touch with reality and talks about strange things like human decomposition or animal mating behaviors. This man is sometimes dangerous; especially, if a woman crosses his very limited boundaries. He may try to "impale" you with his sword if you drop his VHS collection of Spiderman.

The Cheapskate

He treats his dollars better than he treats his woman or his children. He will often take the woman he's courting to the cheapest restaurants, and he's never too fond of leaving a tip.

The Ladies' Man

This guy is a woman's worst nightmare. He has many women calling him, including current girlfriends, friends with benefits, ex-girlfriends, aunties....you name it. He's always busy helping some lady out, and of course, he helps himself to whatever that woman gives him. He is also really good with older women, often gaining their respect and trust. This guy not only loves attention, but he loves praise. Ordinarily, men like this aren't surrounded by a lot of male friends because they are obsessed with women. If you visit their social network pages, you will see that most of their friends are women around their age or younger. They tend to fluctuate from being Christian to being ungodly depending on who they are talking to. This character's significant other is often extremely neglected while he's off helping other damsels in distress.

Mr. Equality

This character is vile in so many ways. He believes in going dutch when dating; he believes in demanding his spouse pay fifty percent of the bills (even when he makes more money), and he does not believe in opening doors for women. This character is often dispassionate, selfish and unfair. Even though he wants to split every responsibility down the middle, he still wants to be the "man of the house" and the decision-maker. Often spoiled by the women in his family, Mr. Equality rarely ever stays married long; finally giving up on marriage and entering a string of dead-end relationships that always end bitterly.

The Professional Prisoner

This guy has been to prison or jail so many

times that he knows the criminal justice system inside out. He's the guy that people call on when they have been brought up on charges. He could be a great guy if he's totally surrendered to GOD, and just giving advice to help others. But if he's still going in and out of prison, he's definitely not marriage material.

Mr. Sow a Seed

This man has sown his seed all around and has many children. He has truly given back to society and is often found in a new relationship every few years, which is the reason he has so many children with so many different women. Again, if he has been delivered and is now serving GOD, he may make a decent husband; nevertheless, if he's still undelivered and fertile, you should stay away from him.

The Quiet Storm

This character is usually very dangerous. In

public view, he's quiet and often stand-offish. At home, he tends to be reclusive; often claiming a room for himself and being very territorial about that room. This man does not like to argue much. Instead, he stores up every problem and every word until he finally snaps. Any woman can easily mistake his quietness as meekness, but make no mistake about it; he burrows every problem he has until he has no more room for it. It's only a matter of time before he's handed a prisoner number, and you don't want to be the reason he got that number.

Conclusion

Of course, there are many unmentioned traits and characters that the women of GOD should be on the lookout for. If you serve GOD by obeying HIM and not looking for a guy, GOD will bless you with Mr. Right in due time. Please don't go around dating men trying to figure out who's who in your life. Anytime a woman sets out to date men, she's basically saying to GOD that she'll find her own husband. Just stay in GOD'S will, and refuse to go out of it. That's the quickest way to drive an Ishmael away. All the same, don't bring men into your life and expect GOD to constantly drive them out. You need to wait on GOD for your husband, not go searching on your own because you feel like GOD is taking too long. Sure, the wait can feel like a long time, and there will be times when you'll think of how ready you are to be found; nevertheless, only GOD knows when your season is upon you. In the meantime, enjoy being GOD'S daughter, and learn to love HIM and yourself so you won't end up getting with any man for the sake of having a man.

Additionally, remember that not all Ishmaels are obvious. Some counterfeit husbands come dressed in some pretty good disguises and won't be discerned by the naked eye or a few conversations. It'll literally take the LORD, through your obedience, to reveal who they are to you. If you slip up even slightly with this character, you may enter a soul tie or a stronghold that can take years and many tears to come out of. Don't be fooled by titles or words. Don't look at how many people are following a man. Remember, Ahab was king and he had a large following. He also had Jezebel by his side. The Pharisees were well respected religious men who had large followings; nevertheless, CHRIST said they were children of the devil. Every kingdom has a king, but you shouldn't try to be the queen unless GOD says so. Otherwise, you may become the queen of a dark kingdom; a place where misery and agony give you a front-row preview of what hell looks and feels like.

Satan's Favorite Weapon

Do you remember the last man you gave your heart to? Do you remember the pain he inflicted on you through it? Do you remember how much it hurt you when that relationship ended? That's because you hadn't done what GOD told you to do. HE said we are to guard (or protect) our hearts. We have to be careful who we allow in our hearts because it is a sacred place. It is our very control center. "Keep thy heart with all diligence; for out of it are the issues of life" (Proverbs 4:23).

Think about the White House. It is considered the heart of the United States because it is the house the President lives in. If you go to the White House, you will find that it's extremely guarded from the outside in. They have to guard the White

House because there are many terrorists who would love to attack and destroy it. Your heart is the same way. There is one big terrorist whose name is Satan, and he owns the largest organization of terrorists in the earth. Just as GOD assigns angels to protect us, Satan assigns devils to attack us. The enemy knows that the most effective way to destroy a believer is by gaining access to their hearts. The heart is our control tower; it is the engine of our lives. Our beliefs are the drivers that get behind the wheels of our hearts and steer us right or steer us wrong. And that's why the enemy sends a man to impersonate your husband. His goal is to get into your heart, and once he's there, he can steer you in the wrong direction.

You'll find that what many lost men do is charm their way into a woman's heart. They'll agree with her on just about everything. They'll hold her, comfort her

and spend every available moment with her.
When you see them together, you think
she's finally found the right man for her.
You stand by in awe of the attention he
showers upon her. But one day, he
suddenly changes. He's now in her heart,
and he has an established soul tie with her,
so he becomes the very opposite of what he
once was. The mask is now off and cloud
nine suddenly evaporates, revealing a long
fall to reality below. She tearfully and
fearfully anticipates the final impact. Even
while still in that relationship, her heart is
broken. It's broken because the wrong man
got in and began to do the works of his
father, the devil. But once he's in, there's
pretty much nothing she can do about it but
pray and wait for GOD to heal her broken
heart. In the meantime, it feels good to her
to keep allowing that man into her heart.
He's the exact size of that giant hole in her
heart, because he's caused it. When he's
there, she can still hope he'll change. When

he's there, she doesn't have to face reality if she doesn't want to. Oftentimes, when a woman loves the wrong man, GOD has to remove that man from her and allow her to grieve. While she's grieving, she has a choice. She can go out there and get another man to take the previous man's place in her heart, or she can invite GOD in so HE can heal her, restore her, guide her and give her understanding.

Your heart is more valuable than the White House. Your heart is a place that's sacred, and it should always remain guarded. Most men who want to enter your life or your bedroom will first try to enter your heart. If the wrong man can get in, he can easily get you to sin against GOD. Satan works overtime trying to link a daughter of Zion up with a son of Baal. Once a man gets into a woman's heart, she will no longer listen to reason or anyone around her. She will believe what she wants to believe because it's comforting to her.

While you prepare for your husband, please guard your heart. I know this isn't always easy because the eyes and ears can be deceptive. You see a beautiful man, and you hear those words you've always wanted to hear. You want to believe what you're hearing because you like what you're looking at. If Satan can enter your heart through your eyes, you were an easy target. Lay every man and his words at the feet of GOD and ask GOD to drive that man and his words away if they are not from HIM. And for the sake of not wasting your time, listen to the voice from within. Some men you don't have to ask GOD about because they are obvious Ishmaels. Sometimes we take the obvious ones before the LORD because they are beautifully wrapped. If you want Mr. Right, get Mr. Wrong away from you as fast as you can. Better yet, don't invite Mr. Wrong anywhere near your ears, and that way, he won't have access to your heart.

Satan's greatest weapon against you is you! Guard your heart; otherwise, a devil will get into your control center and start to overload you with pain. The enemy can't always stop you from getting to where GOD has called you, but he can slow you down.

Be Anxious For Nothing

In the wake of waiting for your husband,
you will find that there are times you'll feel
anxious. You will have waited for a long
time, or it may seem like a long time, and
you will have seen some of your friends
getting married. You'll notice your own
needs, and you will crave the affection,
attention and love you think only a husband
can give, but GOD begs to differ. HE wants
to be everything you want and need, plus
more.

The Bible warns about being anxious.
Philippians 4:6 (NIV) reads, "Do not be
anxious about anything, but in every
situation, by prayer and petition, with
thanksgiving, present your requests to
God."
Why is it that GOD tells us not to be

anxious? To understand this better, we must first get a grasp on what the word "anxious" means. The word "anxious" comes from the Latin word "anxius," which is akin to the Latin word "agere." Agere means: to strangle or choke with anger. Of course, our own definition of "anxious" means to be eager or to show extreme fear; to anticipate with agony. The reason GOD tells us not to be anxious for anything is because we not only put pressure on ourselves when we're anxious, but we are attempting to put pressure on GOD to do what it is that we want. We are putting pressure on HIM to do something HE'S already done, when it is our lack of faith or patience that's keeping us from entering our seasons of receiving. In doing so, we grieve our own souls. You being anxious won't cause GOD to move any faster than HE'S already moving. At the same time, many people still think GOD is "working" on their situation. This implies that HE is a super-busy GOD with all of the problems that are laid on Heaven's throne. The truth is, HE'S already done what HE said HE would do. Once HE spoke it, it was already established. What did HE say in relation to you being found by your husband?

Matthew 6:33: But seek ye first the kingdom of God, and his righteousness; and all these things shall be added unto you.
Note: Have you been seeking HIM first? HE said that if you seek HIM **first**, as well as the Kingdom of GOD and all its righteousness, everything else will be added to you.

John 14:13-14: And whatsoever ye shall ask in my name, that will I do, that the Father may be glorified in the Son. If ye shall ask any thing in my name, I will do it.
Note: Have you even asked HIM for what you want yet? Did you ask in JESUS Name? Will HE be glorified in what you're asking for? You see, women often ask for men

who GOD did not ordain for them to be led by. If GOD were to grant them their petitions, HE would not be glorified. Instead, the enemy would attempt to make a mockery of HIM, and HE will not be mocked. Everything you ask GOD for has to be for your good and HIS glory; otherwise, you ask amiss. Asking GOD for a man who doesn't serve HIM is like asking a police officer to light your crack pipe.

If you've asked and believed GOD for your husband, GOD has already answered you. Now, you are only awaiting the season of manifestation, but you have to be patient to access it. Otherwise, you may abort the process.

There are women out there who anxiously await their husbands, while there are women out there who are simply in waiting. Then again, there are women out there who have learned to stop waiting and start preparing.

The Woman Who Waits Anxiously

A woman who waits anxiously is full of
voids. She's void of wisdom and standing
outside of the will of GOD. Patience or
long-suffering is one of the fruits of the
SPIRIT. You can't approach GOD in a way
that's disrespectful to HIM, and expect HIM
to pacify your attitude. Anytime you find
yourself feeling anxious, you need to open
your Bible and study the book of Proverbs.
You simply need more fuel to get you to the
next day, and the Bread of Life will charge
you up once again. You should also bind the
haughty spirit behind anxiousness. Finally,
you should ask GOD to fill every void in you,
so you don't try to put a man in a place
where only GOD can fit.

A Woman in Waiting

A woman in waiting has gotten somewhat
of an understanding, but she still hasn't fully

matured enough to understand that her wait is over. The word "waiting" implies that you are in a process, and anytime you speak that over yourself, you are saying that the process is continuing. But a woman who understands that GOD has hidden her and placed her so high in HIS heart that only her husband can reach her, is a woman who has been found by her husband. The only thing she's doing now is getting her house and her life together. It's similar to having a husband who's away on a business trip. You know he's your husband, and you know that he'll be back soon. Therefore, you don't wait on him; you prepare for him. Anytime you wait, you will become anxious.

A Woman Who's Preparing

A woman who is preparing for her husband is no longer a woman; she's a wife. She has believed GOD, and her faith has given her access to a place that only a wife can inhabit. She understands that if she's not ready, she will not be found; therefore, she spends every day doing the will of GOD and learning what she needs to learn. One day, she will find herself at the altar with her man of GOD, and as time goes on, she will understand why she had to prepare for her new role. A woman isn't a wife until GOD has called her such. "Whoso findeth a wife findeth a good thing, and obtaineth favour of the LORD" (Proverbs 18:22). You'll notice here that GOD did NOT say "he who finds a woman." HE said "he who finds a wife finds a good thing." The issue is that too many women are looking to be found, when what we should always look to do is find the will of GOD for our lives. We should look to be honored by GOD with the title of "wife" because it is then and only then that we can be found by our GOD-appointed husbands. A woman who marries does not become a wife; she becomes a married woman. And whatever man she marries does not become a husband; he becomes a married man.

Be anxious for nothing, but always remain prayerful. Learn to embrace life as it is, without the husband, so you won't become too needy or clingy when he does find you. A woman who learns to be content with her life will one day be a wife who's content with her husband.

You're Worth the Wait....Is He?

After Jay moved out, we immediately began divorce proceedings. Since we'd shared one car over the course of our marriage, I was left without a vehicle. I let Jay take the vehicle because he had a job that he had to commute to, and I worked from home. I'd saved up some money, and I decided to go and buy my own vehicle.

One day, I went on Craigslist and found a vehicle I liked. I kept coming back to that vehicle, and finally decided to purchase it. I called the owner of the vehicle, but he lived more than two hours away. I had no transportation and did not want to get on a bus with a large sum of money, so I called Jay. Of course, Jay was happy that I was getting a vehicle because that meant I wouldn't fight with him for the vehicle he'd taken. He happily agreed to take me down to the city where the guy and I had agreed to meet so I could purchase the vehicle.

The owner had agreed to meet me halfway, so we drove close to an hour, and waited for him at a bank in that city. We ended up sitting in Jay's car waiting on the man for over an hour. During that time, we began to talk about our pending divorce and why we were divorcing. Jay was surprised that I wasn't bitter towards him, but I spoke to him in love, pleading with him to give his life to the LORD. While talking, Jay said something to me that hurt me, angered me and reassured me all in one. He said to me that I was a good wife and any man would be blessed to have me. He said that he knew he'd never meet another woman like me, and he knew he'd eventually regret ending the marriage. He even asked me if we could possibly remarry someday, and of course, I said no. This statement angered me because it took me back to what my first husband had said. He too told me how good of a woman I was, and how any man that got me would be "lucky." Of course, after we'd broken up, he too tried to reconcile with me, saying I was the best woman he'd ever had. While sitting in that car, I began to cry. Why was it that I was so good, but I just wasn't good enough for the men I'd given my heart and hand to? I had to realize that being good enough wasn't the issue; the issue was, I wasn't bad enough. I didn't like sin, and I was too settled in my mind to entertain a man who wanted to indulge in the sinful pleasures of this world. At the same time, I was and am stubborn. Once my mind is made up, there is no changing it...even with the threat of divorce. I'd made up my mind to serve the LORD, and since I wasn't obedient in getting those men, I had to make the sacrifice of losing them. Remember, obedience is better than sacrifice.

As I sat there crying, I found myself fighting through so many mixed emotions, but the one clear thought I had was that Jay was not the husband for me. I'd spent so much time in both marriages trying to cater to the men I'd married that I had forgotten about myself. I forgot to bless myself. I forgot to love me the way I wanted them to love me. This became obvious as I was living alone. I spent day after day going to fast food restaurants to kill my hunger pains, not considering what kind of damage the food was doing to my body. I didn't think about nourishing my body; I wanted to satisfy it and pleasure my taste buds, so I ate hamburgers, pizza and every unhealthy thing. When I was married both times, I cooked a lot because I wanted to be the best wife I could be. After spending a total of twelve years being married, I found myself living as a single woman and consciously paying attention to my own choices and thoughts. I had to learn to be a better wife alone before I could be a worthy wife to anyone else.

The question is: Was I worth the wait? The obvious answer is: Yes, I am worth the wait for the right man, but I'm not worth it to the wrong one. One of the most valuable lessons I learned about relationships is that you can give your all and be the best wife you can be, but still find yourself in divorce court. Marriage isn't about how good of a wife you are, how much you cook, how good of a cook you are, or how great you are in the bedroom. Just like life, marriage has to be purposeful, and it has to be rooted in the LORD. Too many women get married for the sake of filling voids in their lives or just to have someone to curl up with every night, but they miss the whole point of marriage. Marriage is a GOD-ordained institution arranged by GOD for HIS glory. All too often, we make marriage about us, when it's all about GOD. You see, when you put GOD first, and make GOD the starting point and ending point of your marriage; HE will bless you with a marriage that endures the tests of time. HE will show you why HE is Alpha and Omega; the Beginning and the End.

Are you worth the wait? What do you have to offer to your husband besides great sex and a cooked meal? The better question is: What makes you stand out from other women? Having a ministry and a blog does not make you a valued asset to your husband. What if your husband comes along and he's a millionaire who owns a string of companies and has planted many ministries? What could you help him with besides spending his money and looking good on his arm? Oftentimes, we celebrate our own mediocrities, not understanding that GOD wants to make us greater while we are still single. That way, we can be a blessing to our husbands and not just expect them to come along and lift us up out of our dry places.

When I was going through my first divorce, I was cleaning a room in my house one day when I heard the LORD say to me that I was going to build a website. HE didn't say a man was going to come along and build one for me. HE said I would build that site. I'd spent six years in a marriage where my husband was the larger contributor financially, and I witnessed what it's like to lose almost everything you have once he jumps bail. It was at that time that I realized I was never supposed to depend on him; I was supposed to depend on the LORD.

GOD wants to build you up, provide for you and show you that HE is your husband first. If you don't really understand that HE is your source, you will make an idol of your resource: man, marriage or self. If you don't really understand that greatness is in you, you will always look upon yourself as a nothing who is only something when some man validates you. If you don't really understand how good GOD is, you'll make a great big mess of your life when you keep expecting a man to fill HIS shoes. You are only worth the wait if you are waiting in the LORD. Otherwise, you have devalued yourself, and you need to get back to GOD so you can realize how priceless you are to GOD.

How great of a man do you want to marry? If you're a woman who wants to meet and marry a man who has a large business, financial stability and a never-ending drive for success, you must at least have some business sense, financial stability and a never-ending drive for completion and success. Why? Either you are going to agree and walk with your husband, or you are going to not understand him and walk against him. How can two walk together except they be agreed? Understand it's when two people don't agree that divorce proceedings begin.

Why do you need to have a drive for completion? There are a lot of people who start things, but there are very few who finish them. If you are married to a man who has the drive of a cheetah, you need to be able to catch him in the spirit. In other words, you need to be able to balance him and compliment him, and he ought to do the same for you. You'll notice that when GOD appoints a husband for you, that man's gifts will compliment your own, and when brought together, they will be an anointed explosion of talents.

Woman of GOD, get busy in who are you. You need to get so busy that you forget you're waiting for a husband. Think about your nine to five job. When you're watching the clock, time seems to go by slowly. But when you're busy, time seems to move quickly. It's the same way when you're on GOD'S clock. When you're busy in purpose, you'll suddenly find yourself being courted by the man of GOD that GOD has appointed for you, and this will likely happen when you least expected it. If you're not busy in purpose, you'll find yourself watching the calendar and getting more impatient by the day. If you're not busy in purpose, you'll find yourself settling for the wrong man who does and says the right things.

What about that guy you've given your heart to? Is he worth the wait? If you didn't wait for him, you have your answer already. Any man who leads you into sin is leading you away from GOD. Your GOD-ordained husband will lead you in the LORD, and the two of you will advance in HIM together. One amazing thing I discovered was how much I grew while being married. It wasn't the marriages that grew me up; it was the WORD that grew me up. The more WORD I got in me, the more I began to change into who I was in the LORD. The LORD started giving me more businesses to start, more books to write and more people to help. One day, I looked at the man I was married to and realized he wasn't going anywhere....or at least going anywhere I wanted to go. He wanted to serve his culture, which was a culture rooted in ancestor worship and witchcraft. He wanted to serve his people, but he did not want to serve the LORD. We had different plans for our futures, and I knew and firmly stood on my declaration to him that I was not going to move to his country or involve myself in his culture. I often told him that if he participated in the ancestor worship or the witchcraft, I would have to leave him. Because of this, he rarely spoke with me about his culture and beliefs, and anytime I discovered another appalling fact about his village, he'd just tell me the people were not educated, and that's why they did what they did. Since he often spoke about GOD, I assumed that he was slowly coming around because that's what I wanted to believe.

I'd grown so much, and I was continuing to grow. The more I grew in the LORD, the more distance there was between me and the man I'd married. All I wanted to talk about was GOD, my ministry, business and whatever the LORD had given me to work on. All he wanted to talk about was people. Because of this, we often sat around one another in silence; nevertheless, I continued to wait on him to change.

Do you see what happened here? I'd sinned my way into a marriage, and I still ended up waiting on GOD for my husband; only, I was waiting on GOD for my husband to change. Had I waited as a single woman and let GOD change my mind before I'd met the guy, I wouldn't have had to endure what I endured. The point is...either way you go,

you're going to have to wait. In my case,
the man didn't change, so I ended up
becoming a single woman again. And guess
what? The waiting started all over again,
but this time, I'd made up my mind. I would
NEVER sin against GOD to have a husband
again. There will be no fornication, kissing
or spousal activity occurring between Mr.
Right and I until we've gotten married. I will
not allow him to uncover me naturally until
he covers me spiritually.

So is your guy worth the wait? Do you
realize the horrifying testimonies women
get when marrying the wrong man? If you
think my testimony is piercing, try visiting a
prison and listening to their testimonies.
Try visiting random women and listening to
their testimonies. You'd be amazed what
you'd endure when married to the wrong
man. If the man you have was sent by GOD,
he is worth waiting for. But if he was not
sent by GOD, he was clearly sent by the

devil. Additionally, every Christian man is not your GOD-sent husband.

The funny thing is, the few women I've met who did meet and marry their GOD-ordained husbands will tell any woman that listens about the many Christian men who came after them when they were single. They'd been proposed to, they'd been lied to, and they'd almost made the mistakes of a lifetime. One woman in particular told me a story that has shaped my view of the Christian dating world. I was in my first marriage, and I suspected my husband was having an affair. My husband and her husband were friends, and she and I had become friends. One night, we returned to her apartment, and the guys got out of the vehicle and made their way into the apartment. She and I decided to stay in the vehicle and talk. While we were sitting there, she began to tell me about some of the things her husband had been taking her through. We both began to cry as we shared our stories of infidelities and lies with one another. I will never forget what she said to me. She said that at least I knew my husband was a sinner, so I could expect his behavior from him. But her husband was in the church and preaching against the very things he was doing. I couldn't relate to that pain, even though I was in pain. You see, I felt that if my husband was to get saved, he would change. Hearing her story let me know that salvation does not equal change. Nowadays, one of the questions many women who are in relationships with worldly men ask is if these men could change and become great husbands. As I mentioned earlier, this rarely happens...or it rarely happens with the women they've built a life of sin with. Sure, you can take him to church and teach him what's right, but you can't make him righteous. He has to love GOD and pursue GOD before he can love you and properly pursue you. What's

165

sad is that many women will marry the wrong men and take these guys to church with them. They will have children with those men, and they will wait year after year for their husbands to change. All the same, their husbands will wait year after year for their wives to change back into the sinful characters they portrayed when they were dating and fornicating. One day, reality will set in for each individual within those relationships. The righteous woman will come to realize that the unrighteous man she'd chosen for herself loves his sin more than he loves her. After all, he loves his sin more than he loves the LORD, and that's why he serves sin and not GOD. The unrighteous husband will come to realize that his righteous wife is obviously never going to be the woman he wants her to be. It becomes more and more obvious that she loves the LORD more than she loves her husband (which, by the way, is what she's supposed to do). At this point, both parties will come to a crossroads. They will each decide one final time if they are willing to make that change for the sake of their marriage. In the rare cases that the husband gives himself to the LORD, the marriage will have survived, but his mind still has to be changed; therefore, the road ahead is still pretty bumpy. In most cases, both parties will walk away from one another. The woman will vow to wait on GOD for the next husband, and the husband will vow to never marry again. They waited for nothing. They invested time, money and love into a marriage that was doomed from the start.

Are you willing to wait on the sinner to change, consciously knowing that he may never change? Are you willing to sit back and wait on GOD for your Mr. Right, or will you just settle down with Mr. Right Now? After having seen the GOD-ordained men that GOD has blessed his faithful daughters with, I can truly say that your man of GOD is worth the wait if only you'll wait.

Breaking Up With Mr. Wrong

You have to break up with Mr. Wrong if you ever want to wake up with Mr. Right. Every man who is not your GOD-ordained husband is a roadblock sent by Satan to keep the right man from ever accessing you. He is a distraction, and a fertile one at that. He is a placeholder in your life, and he'll likely jump ship at the first sight of another ship. Sin doesn't win you anything but a trip to the altar for deliverance.

Let's say you are in a relationship with your distraction, and you want to get out of it. First off, one thing you should note is that most, if not all, women who are with the wrong guys are fully aware that their guys are the wrong guys. The problem is, they still think they can find a cure for sin outside of the WORD of GOD. They think they can cure him of his personality. Anyhow, you want to exit the relationship you're in because you know that GOD isn't pleased. What should you do? How can you exit the relationship without drama unfolding, or even worse, someone getting hurt? Below are ten tips that should help.

- Be truthful, not manipulative. As women, we sometimes try to find methods of ending relationships that we feel are better suited for our partners' personalities. These methods often backfire. Tell the truth. You want to serve the LORD and he doesn't. The truth will often help you to end the relationship on a friendlier tone.

- Stop calling the man, and don't take his calls. One of the most dangerous things is to break up with a man but still give him personal access to you. This stops him from getting over you, and it helps that rage to grow in him.

Anytime he calls and you answer, cut the conversation short and talk only about GOD.

- If the two of you live together, it is better that you move out instead of requesting that he moves out. When you are the one ending the relationship, you should be the one making the most sacrifices. Let him keep everything he wants to keep and remain cordial with him.

- Do not accept anymore gifts from him. A man values his money, and whatever he sows his money into is oftentimes viewed as an investment. If he buys something for you, he plans to collect on that investment.

- If he gave you something of value and he wants it back, give it to him. Material things are nothing, and many women have lost their lives trying to hold onto worthless trinkets that couldn't even save their lives.

- Pray him out. This is an obvious one that most women never think to consider. Ask GOD to remove your boyfriend so HE can send your husband. Ask HIM to remove the guy peacefully and cause the two of you to forgive one another as you transition.
- Obey him out. One of the quickest ways to get rid of the wrong man is to serve GOD in every area of your life. An unholy man hates holiness. Ask GOD to lead you, and just obey everything HE tells you to do, no matter how strange it may seem.
- Lead him out. One thing about men is that they are born to lead and hate to be led by a woman. Simply have Bible study with him every day and tell him what each scripture means. At the same time, continue to lead others to CHRIST. He'll likely get bored and agree with you that the

relationship is going nowhere fast.

- Fill your home and your life with righteous people who love to talk about the LORD. A sinner craves to be around people like himself, and will often feel uncomfortable amongst believers. Surround yourself with believers, and always keep GOD first. Additionally, if he invites his sinful friends over, the quickest way to stop them from visiting is to buy multiple Bibles and have Bible study with them every time they come over.

- Absolutely refuse to sin...period! Don't fornicate with him, don't drink with him, don't gamble with him....only do what GOD wants you to do. Oftentimes, worldly men will try to drag sin out of you even if they have to aggravate it out of you. Instead of cursing him out when he goes above and beyond to hurt you, try blessing him.

One thing about righteousness is that it repels the devil, but it attracts the LORD. "Submit yourselves therefore to God. Resist the devil, and he will flee from you. Draw nigh to God, and he will draw nigh to you" (James 4:7-8). I personally know this to be true because GOD began to order my steps towards the beginning of my marriage to Jay. Once we moved in together, I went between serving GOD and serving my feelings. After a while, I began to listen to the instruction of the LORD more and more. GOD began ministering to me in good times and bad times. HE told me what to do for Jay. HE told me to apologize to Jay even when I wasn't wrong. HE told me to buy Jay a gift even when he was mistreating me. HE told me to tell Jay that I loved him even when he acted unlovable. I watched the atmosphere break in my home many times because of my obedience to GOD. At the same time, I witnessed a man who could no longer launch up-to-date accusations

174

against me begin listing issues I thought we'd made peace with in the past. I stopped being the guilty party, and when I did, I didn't have to do a thing. All I had to do was sit back and watch the WORD work.

When you serve GOD with your whole heart, oftentimes, you won't have to break it off with Mr. Wrong. He'll break it off with you. "And I will cause the captivity of Judah and the captivity of Israel to return, and will build them, as at the first" (Jeremiah 33:7).

Obedience is Better than Sacrifice

I ended up having a dream one night after I had become a single woman again. In that dream, there were two very handsome men who were interested in me. There was an ex-boyfriend from my past, who I would never consider rekindling a relationship with, and there was a guy I'd never seen before. The ex-boyfriend started ignoring me, but he continued to hang around my family. He was upset with me because he'd somehow made it clear that he required premarital sex, and I wasn't giving in. He stuck around my family so he could be a present force in my life, but he ignored me, hoping it would cause me to give in.
The other guy was quiet and mysterious. He seemed more mature, and his desires weren't immediately known. I just assumed he would respect my vow of celibacy.

In the dream, I went someplace with him, and in every room, there were beds. We sat on the bed and talked a little, and I marveled at how handsome he was. I felt that if I could only have him for myself, I'd be one happy woman.

While we were in the first room, another person came into the room and started looking around. We decided to move to the next room so we could be alone. In the next room, there were several beds, all covered in white linen. The man in my dreams (not of) sat on one bed and I sat on the next one. At first, he sat on one of the beds across from me, but after I started speaking with him, he moved over next to me. While I was talking to him, he suddenly leaned in to kiss me. This took me by surprise because we hadn't formally established that we were courting, even though we were both flirting with one another. I didn't resist him, however. I began to return his kisses, even though in

the dream, I began to remember my vows
to GOD. After my separation from Jay, I'd
vowed I wouldn't even kiss a man until our
wedding day. Now, here I was in the dream
kissing a man. I began to reason with
myself that kissing wasn't all that bad, so
after not kissing him back for a few seconds,
I finally kissed him back. Suddenly, I noticed
that he'd started trying to French kiss me,
and that's when I decided that I needed to
make things clear with him. In the heat of
that moment, I'd told myself that kissing
was okay, but I definitely wasn't going to
have sex before marriage. I pushed him
away, and he went and sat back on the bed
across from me. The man in my dreams
(not of) sat on one bed and I sat on the next
one staring at one another. I finally let it
out. I said, "Look, I am celibate and I'm
going to remain celibate until marriage. I
hope you're okay with that." He leaned
back on the bed he was sitting on, and his
eyes seemed to change from being

mysterious and compassionate to being familiar and dispassionate. He responded, "No, I'm not okay with that." And with that, I knew the relationship was over.

When I woke up, I thought about the dream a few times, and then the LORD gave me understanding. The guy from my past represented the obvious men who wanted sex, and the obvious familiar spirits associated with our pasts. He represented my past and what was behind me. Even in the dream, I would not give him a second chance because I was determined to move forward with my life.

The other guy was not familiar to me initially. He wasn't so obvious at first, and instead of asking to bed me or making his intentions for me more clear, he made a move on me. Because I had not considered that he could cross the line with me, I was unprepared. And I obviously wasn't rooted too well in my "no kissing" clause because I began to reason with myself as to why kissing was okay, even as I noticed him attempting to round third base.

Once I made it clear, however, that I would not sin against GOD, his eyes changed and he became familiar. He was a well-disguised familiar spirit, and obedience caused his cover to be blown.

There were two messages that I got from this dream. There is a man, or a type of man, that we're familiar with because of the men from our pasts. We've learned how to discern "his kind" and we stay away from them because it's obvious what they want. It doesn't matter what tactics they try, we remain firmly placed in our convictions, and we continue forth without him. But there's also a man who wears a mask. He appears to be everything we want in a husband, and we secretly wish to have him for ourselves. Oftentimes, we want him simply because of the skin he's wrapped in. This guy is mysterious to us at first, and we stick around him because we've filled out the blanks of the mystery ourselves. We tell ourselves that he is the one who we'll marry. Why? Because he's cute and mysterious. We even ignore our surroundings; surrounding that make his intentions with us clearer. In my dream, I was in bedrooms with Mr. Mystery man. We will begin to reason with ourselves, often lowering our standards so we can have that great man of mystery. Nevertheless, obedience will find him out, expose him and cause him to distance himself from us.

What's the message here? Stick by your convictions, and don't be so easily swayed by the element of mystery. A familiar spirit will disguise itself so that it won't be so familiar to you. "And no marvel; for Satan himself is transformed into an angel of light" (2 Corinthians 11:14).

Make a list of what you will and won't do, and lay that list before the LORD. Ask GOD to give your GOD-ordained husband the same convictions, or at least let him have respect for your convictions. You'd be amazed at how many times you would have fallen for the wrong man, but the revealing of the spirit behind that man was made known because of your obedience and the requirements you laid before the LORD. You see, many people have requirements that they have not taken to GOD, so other people are able to talk them into relaxing their standards a little. But once you've taken that list before the LORD, you should never allow anyone to tell you otherwise. Let GOD prove them wrong. The right man will be able to withstand because he will recognize who you are for him. The wrong man will try to negotiate with you because he wants to see what you can be for him. In other words, he wants to try you on for size. There are many women who sacrifice their standards, rather than sacrificing those wrongful relationships before they even start. As women, we tend to look at the man's appearance, his dress code, his job, his finances and his relationship status. If he looks good, dresses well, has a decent-paying job and is single, most single women would give him a go. And that's why it's so easy for Satan to send a well-dressed devil their way.

Always remember that every sacrifice is something you'll want, but you're sacrificing it to get what you both need and want. Sure, you can settle down with the beautiful Hector who drives the Mercedes Benz and works as a dentist. Sure, Hector would look good on your arms for a while, and people would marvel at the sight of you driving Hector's car. Sure, Hector's marriage proposal may be elaborate and one your town will never forget. But is Hector the one GOD chose for you? Because if he isn't, you are disobeying GOD and you have laid GOD'S plans for you on the altar to be sacrificed. What you don't realize, however, is that Satan has plans for you, and he's already set them in motion with Hector. Hector may end up being the most beautiful and agonizing mistake you've ever made. Consider Abraham and Lot. When Abraham decided to part ways with Lot, he let Lot choose the direction he'd go in, and Lot saw how beautiful the Jordan Valley was. Lot ended up going to Sodom in the way of the Jordan, and we all know what happened from there. GOD destroyed Sodom and Gomorrah, and Lot's wife turned into a pillar of salt because she disobeyed GOD and looked back. The point is, every way that looks good isn't necessarily the right way. The Bible says that Lot saw that everything towards the Jordan Valley was well-watered. Abraham likely went in the way of the desert, but GOD was with him and he was blessed. "And the LORD said

185

unto Abram, after that Lot was separated from him, Lift up now thine eyes, and look from the place where thou art northward, and southward, and eastward, and westward: For all the land which thou seest, to thee will I give it, and to thy seed for ever. And I will make thy seed as the dust of the earth: so that if a man can number the dust of the earth, then shall thy seed also be numbered. Arise, walk through the land in the length of it and in the breadth of it; for I will give it unto thee" (Genesis 13:14-17). What's the difference between Lot and Abraham? Lot looked at the land, but Abraham looked at his GOD. You could be like a "lot" of women and look at Hector, or you can be that rare diamond who keeps her eyes on GOD despite what others say and do. Unfortunately, the woman who ends up with Hector will end up with a testimony that she didn't have to have.

Know this: The enemy will send many well-dressed bachelors your way, and these men may look like the cream of the crop. But if you'll simply walk away and not even give these guys a chance, or let your curiosity venture off with them, you will have laid the right sacrificial offering on the altar. If you don't, you'll be sacrificing your standards, and eventually, that relationship will take itself to the altar and commit suicide.

In Storage

When my first husband left, I remained in our home for about another six to nine months. After that, I lost the house to foreclosure. When I moved my things out, I put just about everything we had together in storage, I moved in with a friend of mine, and eventually moved back home with my mother. My friend and I were both going through divorces, and I felt that she would better understand the transitioning I was going through.

Every month, I paid that storage bill because I did not want to lose my furniture or personal possessions. Even after Jay and I got married, I still had my old furniture in storage. I eventually sold everything I had before I moved to Germany to be with Jay. I remember how freeing it felt to get rid of all that stuff because it linked me to my first marriage.

Once Jay and I separated, I found myself in our old apartment with all of our old things. Every piece of furniture I possessed had a memory of Jay attached to it, even though most of those memories weren't good ones. I remembered how we'd chosen the dining room table. I wanted a different table, but Jay wanted that table because it was on clearance. I eventually grew to love the table, however. We'd chosen the sofa because it too was on sale. Jay came home from work one day with an ad for the sofa, and told me we could get it the next day. I liked it, so I agreed. I didn't know where he got the money from to purchase it, but I learned to stop asking questions every time he came up with money because he'd always say he borrowed it. After that, he'd withhold money and say he had to pay the person back that he borrowed it from. But if I didn't ask questions, he never seemed to owe anyone back.

As I was going through our old apartment, I felt this peculiar nudge to organize and purge the apartment. I knew that it was GOD, so I began offering Jay everything I associated mostly with him, and he took some of it. Whatever he didn't want, I trashed. I had taken so much stuff to the side of the road because I wanted the apartment to be my own for the short time I'd be in it.

One day, I was in Walmart buying some items to organize my apartment when I came onto the bedding aisle. I saw a comforter that I adored, so I bought it. I wasn't in the market for a comforter, but I felt like I had to buy it. I'd stopped sleeping in the bed I once shared with Jay, and was now sleeping on the sofa. I thought the comforter would make it easier for me to sleep in that bed.

The next day, I went to wash my new comforter and sheets. Once the bedding was washed and dried, I took it to the bedroom to put it on my bed, but suddenly realized that putting new covers on that mattress was like putting clean underwear on a dirty woman. At that moment, I felt a pull on me to get rid of the old mattress and buy a new one. I decided in my heart that I'd get up the next day and buy a new mattress for my bed. I even got rid of the pillows.

Once my new mattress arrived and I put my new comforter and pillows on it, it felt like a different bed. Truthfully, I could not remember sleeping that good for a long time. That's when I realized why I didn't sleep in that room. I'd told myself that it was because the bed was so big, and it felt strange for me to sleep in it alone. But that wasn't the case. The issue was that the bed was the marriage bed of Jay and I, and it felt strange to sleep in it without him. Jay was physically gone, but he was still very much present in that room and I couldn't stand to go in it.

There are a few things I want to touch on, and they are:
- Storage
- Foreclosure- Saving
- Closure
- Replace

Storage

When I had items in storage, I knew there was nothing I would be able to do with them if I planned to marry again. No red-blooded American man would allow me to bring my old furniture into a marriage with him. After all, another man had purchased and enjoyed that furniture. Truthfully, if a man didn't mind me keeping it, I would not have wanted that man.

The same goes for the heart. Oftentimes,

we store up our old ways and keep them for whatever relationships we enter. We think all the good we did for one man will be appreciated by the next man, when that just isn't true. Each man is his own man. When you get married, you and your husband should build together. You should never bring mindsets from your past into the marriage. That's why it's important to heal, release and be released before we are found by our GOD-appointed husbands. I remember cooking foods for Jay that I used to cook for my previous husband, and Jay didn't like them. He had his own menu, and I had to learn to cook the foods that he liked.

As women, we tend to pack up those old recipes and our mindsets and we await the man who'll appreciate them. But the truth is, anytime you get married, you are supposed to enter that marriage as a virgin. I do understand that the large majority of

people who get married aren't virgins;
nevertheless, that's why it's important for
us to get delivered from those soul ties and
the mindsets birthed of those soul ties. We
have to be made new again so we don't
bring old baggage into a new relationship.
We have to be trusting again. We can't
memorize the signs of a man cheating just
because the former man cheated;
otherwise, we'll cut an innocent man down
because of our insecurities. We can't break
the relationship up easily just because
we've seen that behavior in a man before,
and we are determined not to go back
down that road. Every man is different.

Imagine this: You meet and court a man
who eventually steals your heart. He treats
you better than you've ever been treated by
a man. He asks you to marry him, and you
happily accept.
After the wedding, you move into his house
with him and find it already furnished. The

furniture is nice, but it's not your style. You want to replace it with new furniture, but he's against it because he says that he and his former wife worked hard to pay for that furniture. He takes you into the bedroom and points to the right side of the bed, and he says to you, "That was my ex-wife's side of the bed, so that will be your side of the bed. This is my side." How would you feel? Would you sleep in that house, let alone, in that bed? The majority of women would scream a resounding "no." That bed, that house and that furniture has been marked by the previous woman. That's her territory. Even though she's physically gone, she's still there.

Isn't that what we do with relationships? We bring in old ways of thinking that were developed from our highs and lows with other men, and we tell our new guys what we will or won't tolerate based on what the previous men did. We try to structure our lives with the new husbands by making sure we have room to fit in all of the hurts and lessons we've learned from the old guy. It's simple. We often destroy new relationships with old ones.

Get rid of:

- The hurt you once felt.
- The material things that link you to the past guy or guys.
- The clothing and under garments you wore when you were intimate with guys from your past.
- The friendships established in your pain that link you to that pain.

Stop storing up things and people and trying to bring them through those opened doors that GOD has anointed you to go through. You can't go through any doors GOD has opened for you until you close the doors you opened for yourself.

Foreclosure

Ordinarily, foreclosure is the repossessing of a home by a bank or mortgage company due to the mortgagor's failure to pay the mortgage.

In this section, however, foreclosure is the repossessing of who you are due to your previous guy's inability to pay the price required to be with you. When I lost my first home to foreclosure, I wasn't aware that the bank had foreclosed on my home. I thought they'd send me a notice of eviction, but they didn't. A man had come to the house, and he was supposed to look the house over for the bank. When he went in, he found the house fully furnished, and he went out of his way to reach me. I was at work at the time, and he told me that if the bank knew I still had stuff in that house, they'd take possession of it all. After that house had been foreclosed on, everything that was in that house was now the legal property of the bank. It was only the favor of GOD that set things in motion where that particular guy ended up coming to my place. He allowed me to get my possessions out of it, and that was when I put them in storage.

Anytime we enter relationships, we lose a large part of who we are because we learn to become who our husbands or male friends want us to be. This is why so many women start "finding themselves" after a relationship ends. They have to go back out and repossess themselves before they can truly move forward. Unfortunately, a large number of women never stake claim to their real identities because they stay hung up on the man who convinced them to let go of those identities. Let's face it. He's gone. That man was not your husband, and he has evicted you from his heart. Renounce that soul tie and find yourself again.

The more you find of yourself, the more you'll discover just how much of yourself you lost in those previous relationships. What is it that you like to do? What haven't you done in a long time? Get out and do it. Get out and repossess yourself, and do not mark yourself down for another man. Wait on GOD. HE will bless you with a better man than you could have even imagined for yourself. "Now unto him that is able to do exceeding abundantly above all that we ask or think, according to the power that worketh in us" (Ephesians 3:20).

Closure

The purpose of a memory is to:

- Remind you of what GOD has brought you through.
- Remind you of your choices and their consequences.
- To testify to others.

The purpose of an imagination is to:

- Show you what GOD can do for you.
- To show you what you have done to

yourself.

Anytime a relationship ends, closure is needed to press forward. But there are some things that keep us from getting the closure that we need, and they oftentimes have everything to do with our minds. As women, we tend to spend a lot of time in our memory banks and our imaginations. This leaves us little time to deal with reality. Because of this, we imagine ourselves with our husbands or guy friends for an eternity. We imagine them being the loving, protective and providing creatures that great memories are made of. We live in a fantasy world, and when we come back to reality, we are often trying to organize what's real around what's imagined. Then, one day, the men we've chosen for ourselves hurt us, and some even walk away. Rather than forgiving them, we sit there in the ruins of our imaginations and we tap into our memories. We remember all the good we've done, and we remember all the bad they've done in return. From there, bitterness begins to form, and we begin to imagine the falls of the men who've single-handedly destroyed our Utopias.

What's amazing is that most women learn to function from within a broken place. So, we're off and about smiling and enjoying life, all the while, our hearts are in ruins. We meet another man, and we want to invite him into our hearts, but because it's a messy place, we shower him with words of love to distract him anytime he tries to get anywhere near our hearts. If he marries us, he's dragged kicking and screaming into his own little cell in a hideous heart that was well hidden behind a beautiful smile. Now, he must serve time and pay the price for another man's crimes.

In order for anyone to function in a

relationship, they must have closure from the relationships of their past. Most relationships end because one or both parties dragged in the corpses of their past relationships.

Ordinarily, when a person hears the word "closure", they think of a conversation they must have with the person who broke their hearts. The truth is, if someone has broken your heart in the past, you should never open up to them. In order to have a conversation with them, you have to open up your heart to them, and they'll sort through what you have in your heart. They may still call the lies truth, and the truth lies, and this will only confuse you. What you'll discover about a liar is that he lies, even when there's no reason for him to lie. A liar lies just because he wants to see how you'll respond to the lie or how good of a liar he is. A liar should never be anywhere near your heart.

To get closure, you must first get an understanding. Understand why your relationship failed. Understand what you did wrong, even from the beginning. Understand that the relationship wouldn't have worked, no matter how much you invested in it. If GOD wasn't in it, you shouldn't have been in it. Anyone who does not get closure ends up with a zip code in unforgiveness. My closure came when I told myself:

- It wasn't my ex-husbands' faults. They were worldly, and I went into the world in search of them. It's not like they came masquerading as angels of light. I should have known better and I should have waited on GOD.
- They only did what they knew how to do. How dare I expect them to do otherwise!
- I was once broken myself, and I hurt people when I was in the midst of my

own pain.

- If they repented, GOD forgave them. It would be silly of me not to do the same.
- They still have some great characteristics about them, and I learned from both of those marriages.
- When I was lost, GOD found and changed me. HE can do the same for them.

In wishing them the best, I learned to forgive, let go and be the woman GOD created me to be.

Replace

Sure, you can't replace the old guy with a new guy, but you can replace those plans of yours with a new vision. Sometimes, the very thing that holds us to our pasts is the plans we once had for our futures. What if you were an architect and someone handed you two separate notebooks full of notes? In one notebook, they have the plans for their old vision. In the other notebook, they have the plans for their new vision. You ask them which notes they want you to work with, and they say they want you to take the both of them and just be creative. As a professional, you know this design is not going to come together because it's two different visions. You want to work with the current vision because it represents what the client wants now, but the old vision represents what the client wanted some time ago.

You work hard and long to put that vision together, and it ends up looking awful, but it's what the customer wants. You call the customer and they come out and view the design you've put together. Even though it's no beauty, they decide to go forward with it because it includes everything they wanted. Once the design is put together, the customer begins to berate you. What in the world were you thinking? How could you put together such an ugly design?!

The customer is living in the new structure, and nothing seems to function the way they want it to. They have to walk from the kitchen through the garage to get to the living room, but hey, it was their idea. Their bathroom is also next to their kitchen, so along with the smell of his wife's cooking filling the air, he has to smell his teenage son's daily bathroom runs. This customer goes on to badmouth you and costs you many clients.

You're probably reading that and finding yourself aggravated with the customer, but that is EXACTLY what we do to GOD. We bring HIM plans that include ideas from our past along with visions for our future, and we expect HIM to create some masterpiece from it. If HE were to answer our prayers, and give us the desires of our hearts, we then call ourselves upset with HIM. The issue is that we forgot to let go of yesterday so we could grab a hold of today.

As a graphic designer, I have had my share of customers like that. They bring me a logo from their past, and it is hideous. For whatever reason, they love that hideous logo. Maybe their son or daughter designed it for them some years ago. Maybe they designed it for themselves. Or maybe some graphic designer had a problem with them and threw together a design to reflect how he or she felt about them. Whatever reason it may be, that customer wanted to keep that logo and merge it with whatever design I was to put together. I would tell the customer that the design is low resolution and would not look good on his new design; nevertheless, he may insist that I use it. In my case, I tell the customer to find another designer because I know how that story is going to end. I'm not going to waste my time putting together a design that the customer is not going to like, and even worse than that, a design that will haunt my portfolio for generations to come.

GOD wants you to let go of all of those plans, ideas and visions that you birthed in those relationships, and let HIM give you a better plan. "There are many devices in a man's heart; nevertheless the counsel of the LORD, that shall stand" (Proverbs 19:21).

So, you and Hector planned to open a car wash together, but now that Hector's gone, you still want to go forth with that car wash. What you're doing is bringing Hector into whatever relationship you enter. I truly understand how hard it is to let go of a vision you build with another man, especially one that you were excited about, but in order to embrace GOD'S plans for you, you have to release your plans for yourself. The only plans you can keep are the ones GOD has for you.

Think of a car. Let's say a woman was told by her mechanic that she needed a new headlight, but she's fond of her old headlight too. She requests that the mechanic leave the old headlight in the vehicle...maybe taping it to the new headlight. How crazy would she sound? The old headlight is gone and has to be replaced, but she still wants to hold on to it because she says it once shined brighter than a noon day. Maybe it will wake up and shine again.

Go to GOD with a clean slate, and ask HIM to make you over. Ask HIM to cause you to walk in HIS plans for you. Whatever it is that HE has purposed you to do, you will find excitement in it. Don't go to GOD with all of those plans you've picked up along the way, asking HIM to bless them. That's like bringing that old furniture into your new husband's house and asking him to dust them off. You don't have to replace a thing; GOD will replace it.

And before I go any further, let me say this. I know that many of you will look at how I was able to get up and replace things like the mattress, car and some of the furniture. You'll say that you don't have the money to do those things; therefore, you believe your situation to be one that has to be approached differently. When we are in soul ties, we often look for any reason to say our situations are different; therefore, we have to find another approach. That's because we often want to remain in those relationships or hold on to those things that have held us in bondage. "I freed a thousand slaves. I could have freed a thousand more if only they knew they were slaves." ~Harriet Tubman

Saving money was part of my foreclosure.

While Jay and I were married, he wanted separate accounts. Jay paid the majority of the bills; I only paid the cell phone bill and bought the groceries. I learned to build the businesses GOD gave me and to save money, using most of it as an investment back into my businesses and ministries. GOD started preparing me to be a single woman while I was still married, and I didn't realize it at the time. My businesses grew, my ministry grew, and my finances grew...right under Jay's nose. He didn't have access to my account because he assumed he was the breadwinner. You see, when you get busy in purpose and do what GOD has told you to do, HE will show you that HE'S a far better husband than any man could ever be to you. HE'S a far better friend than any person could be to you. I personally tasted disobedience and I found it to be bitter and harmful. I personally tasted and saw that the LORD is good, and I found HIM to be faithful and wonderful.

Romans 8:28: And we know that all things work together for good to them that love God, to them who are the called according to his purpose.

Psalm 34:8: O taste and see that the LORD is good: blessed is the man that trusteth in him.

The Importance of Identification

I went to the gym the other day, and because I entered through the main door, I was stopped and asked for identification. After I officially joined the gym, they showed me a back door where I'd be entering from that day forth. They can easily distinguish members from non-members based on the door they enter. Members have a key; non-members don't have keys. And it's like that in many of the places you'll find yourself in that require a membership. You have to show some identification to prove you have the right to be there. What about your heart?

The heart is like a high security building, but it's only guarded by you...an imperfect being. That's why so many trespassers have successfully made it past your judgment and entered your heart, where they did unspeakable damage. Each trespasser was a lesson designed to teach you to better guard your heart. It goes without saying, however, that some people get past your judgment because they look or speak a certain way.

It is very important to learn to distinguish Isaac from Ishmael, otherwise, you'll keep letting your eyes and ears work as security, and they don't make great guards. A woman doesn't become a wife until she learns to guard her heart the way a lioness guards her cubs. Instead of measuring a man by what you want on the outside, it is better to weigh him by the WORD he has on the inside. Is he HOLY GHOST filled? Does he love the LORD with his whole heart? Is his light shining, or does his light only shine on Sundays? Please understand that Ishmael comes in an array of personalities and faces, but you can't entertain your desire to date him just to see where the relationship goes. As women, we often date men who are obviously not for us just because they look good, sound good, or they drive nice cars.

It is very important to learn to discern who should be in your life and who should not. Additionally, you need to learn where everyone is to be positioned in your life. For example, GOD may send a man into your life to receive a WORD from you, but because that man is cute and Christian, you may assume he's your GOD-sent husband. Sure, he's GOD-sent, but he wasn't sent to be your husband. GOD had another purpose for you in that man's life. Anytime a man needs to learn the WORD from you, he is clearly not your husband, since the husband is to be the head of the home. Sure, your husband will learn from you sometimes, but he needs to be able to teach you most of the time. It's hard for a woman to respect a man who knows less than she does, and it's hard for a man to love a woman who does not respect him.

Ephesians 5:22-33: Wives, submit yourselves unto your own husbands, as unto the Lord. For the husband is the head of the wife, even as Christ is the head of the church: and he is the saviour of the body. Therefore as the church is subject unto Christ, so let the wives be to their own husbands in every thing.

Husbands, love your wives, even as Christ also loved the church, and gave himself for it; That he might sanctify and cleanse it with the washing of water by the word, That he might present it to himself a glorious church, not having spot, or wrinkle, or any such thing; but that it should be holy and without blemish. So ought men to love their wives as their own bodies. He that loveth his wife loveth himself. For no man ever yet hated his own flesh; but nourisheth and cherisheth it, even as the Lord the church: For we are members of his body, of his flesh, and of his bones. For this cause shall a man leave his father and mother, and shall be joined unto his wife, and they two shall be one flesh. This is a great mystery: but I speak concerning Christ and the church. Nevertheless let every one of you in particular so love his wife even as himself; and the wife see that she reverence her husband.

Learning Ishmaels' many faces is vital to your purpose. Ishmael is a weapon formed against you, and he will prosper if you open your heart to him. The plan of the enemy is to station one of his sons in your heart, because it is there that he can do the most damage. You know what you don't want in a husband, and you know the signs that a man is not the right man. Satan is aware of this, but he is also aware of your voids. He knows most women will settle for a man who fills her voids and pleasures her eyes and ears. In other words, the enemy uses your five senses (flesh) against you. After a few sweet lies and the flash of a deceitful, but beautiful smile, Ishmael has caused many women to began reasoning with themselves. All of a sudden, a woman's words change when Ishmael is on the scene. Many women will go from saying they refuse to kiss a man until their wedding day, to saying there's nothing wrong with kissing. This is a clear indication that Ishmael is on the scene, and he's getting a passing grade on his demonic assignment. That's why it is a good idea to write down what you want in a husband and know what GOD has in store for you in a husband. Anytime you begin to reason with yourself, you are likely dealing with Ishmael.

In preparing for Mr. Right, you also need to know you more. The more you know about you, the more you'll learn about Mr. Right.

For example, if you know that you don't fare well in relationships where you don't get a lot of affection and attention, you'll easily identify some of the Ishmaels who approach you just by looking at them or listening to them. Sometimes, it's easy to discern Ishmael just from a glance. Other times, a few conversations will be enough to turn the light on in your discernment. And there are those times when prayer is needed because the man who is pursuing you seems to have all of his ducks in a row. Truthfully, the issue is that many single women are a little too anxious to be married, and this opens the door for a well-disguised Ishmael.

In getting to know you more, you'll learn so many different facets to your personality, and these revelations aren't just clues as to who you are, but they will serve as clues as to who is and who is not your GOD-appointed husband. Nevertheless, to get to know you better, you must first get to know the LORD better. Who you are is so hidden in HIM that it is revealed to you only when you diligently search out HIS heart.

Finally, you need to identify the areas in your heart that need to be guarded the most. You do this by identifying what it is you want in a husband right now. What you want in a husband oftentimes reflects what you believe you are missing in your life. For example, let's say you want a husband because you want someone to cook for, sleep with and someone to help you with that mounting debt. In having those types of voids and issues, you are not seeking a husband; you are seeking a man to take GOD'S place in some areas of your life and a husband to take your current husband's place in other areas of your life. The areas in your life that needs to be guarded are whatever areas those voids stem from, and you need to learn to be GOD dependent, and not man dependent. You have to guard those areas with faith, and to get this faith, you need the WORD of GOD. Therefore, in looking for someone to cook for, you are looking to mother someone or something. Maybe you have children and you're not mothering them in certain areas, causing you to have that urge to pour out, but you think you need to pour out in a man. Think about an animal who loses its children. Instinct tells that animal that she is a mother and should be nursing, so she may go out and try to mother any abandoned animals she may come across. That's why you'll find dogs nursing kittens and lionesses nursing fawns. They still have milk in their breasts; therefore, they want to do what their instincts tell them to do and that is to nurture a baby. Many women do the same. Some of our parents didn't nurture us in certain areas, so when we became parents, we didn't nurture our children in those areas either. Nevertheless, there was still that desire there to nurture someone in that area, and oftentimes, women give this leftover milk to men. Then again, any woman who has had sex before is considered a wife by GOD. Until she allows GOD to sever that soul tie and put that marriage asunder, she will have that desire to do the things a wife does, and she'll often do that with the men in her life. For example, you'll see women who love to cook for any man who comes into their homes, be they boyfriends, uncles, cousins or nephews. When women come to visit them, on the other hand, they don't cook. They need to nurture someone or something because their souls tell them they are married, and they often associate that someone or something with a man.

Additionally, if you want to get married to have someone to sleep with or to have legal sex with, this is a clear indication that you are still married to some man. When the

224

soul is tied up in a soul tie, the mind responds accordingly. Your soul says you are married, but your understanding says you are single. Your faith says you can't sleep with a man until you are legally married, but your body cries out for sex. In this, confusion sets in and you'll find yourself wanting to be married for all the wrong reasons. In other words, you are an uncovered wife looking for a covering. In order for you to be free, you have to repent of past fornications and ask GOD to sever those unions. Only GOD can divide or divorce your soul from a man.

Lastly, if you want to get married because of mounting debt, you are completely out of order. What you're saying is you're looking for a man to come in and take that burden off your shoulders, when CHRIST told you to cast every burden upon HIM. Again, in such thinking, you are looking for a man to come in and fill the LORD'S shoes.

In identifying your needs, you can easily learn to cast those needs upon the LORD so HE can meet them. That way, when your husband finds you, he doesn't find a beautiful pile of a woman waiting to be sifted through. Instead, he will find a woman after GOD'S own heart; one he can wear as a crown and glorify the Name of the LORD.

Secretly Single

One of the things I've noticed with a lot of single Christian women is that they constantly advertise the fact they are single. When the enemy sees this, he knows they are in the market for a husband. Many women say they want "the" husband GOD has for them, but in truth, many women just want a man who's Christian and working.

One of the dilemmas I faced when Jay and I broke up was whether or not I should go public with our breakup. After all, I'd written many marriage self-help books and helped many mend the broken places in their marriages. I eventually did post it once the LORD gave me permission to do so, and I gave a public notice to the enemy that his plans would not discredit my ministry. But I worried about single men (Christian and non-Christian) seeing that post. I didn't want any men fueling up their vehicles of pursuit and coming after me. So besides giving my testimony about how I'd disobeyed GOD in choosing a man and the results that followed, I refrained from posting anything else about my new relationship status. I decided I wanted to remain secretly single.

A lot of women think they need to be seen and heard in order to be found by their husbands, and this is not true. The best place to be is hidden in the LORD. You don't have to make it known that you are single and waiting. You shouldn't look at every cute guy and imagine him being the one for you. You shouldn't look at every average or below-average guy and wonder if you need to lower your standards. Sure, the enemy will say to you that the reason you're single is because your standards are too high, but all of the men worth having are the men you aren't interested in. Don't over-think it. You should be so busy in the LORD that you don't have too much idle time to let your mind wander off. Let GOD clean you up and HE will take you into your season to be found. HE doesn't need your help. All HE needs you to do is be obedient to HIM and stay busy in purpose. The problem with many women is that they believe their purpose is wrapped up in a man, when in truth, their purpose will tie to their husband's purpose perfectly. What if GOD were to let that man find you while you are not in purpose, but he is? You'd become a distraction to that man, often complaining that he's not spending enough time with you. But if that man finds you not only purposeful, but purpose-driven, you won't be a distraction; you'll be a help meet.

Start being faithful to your husband now. Don't run around dating men and taking notes. Every time you go and find your own guy, you are saying to GOD that you will do HIS job for HIM. Once you find one you want to marry, you'll likely run back before HIM and tell HIM that you're getting married. After the wedding and a dose of reality, you'll be back in front of the Throne asking GOD to change your husband. This is a pattern that happens with many believing women. JEHOVAH (YAHWEH) is our FATHER; therefore, we shouldn't approach HIM and tell HIM who we are going to marry. We should always approach HIM and ask HIM to tell us who this guy is that's pursuing us. Did he come from you, LORD? Or did he come from the enemy? When GOD sees that you are involving HIM in your decisions, and you are allowing HIM to be the decision-maker for you, HE won't let you down.

Dress Code
As a Christian woman, you should always

dress respectfully, and never wear clothes that tempt any man to lust after you. At the same time, you should practice being the respectable woman a respectable man will want to have on his arm. Too many women in the church overdo it. Extra long wigs, fake lashes, fake fingernails and a ton of makeup. Don't get me wrong, there's nothing wrong with wanting to look good, but there is such a thing as overdoing it. You know you've overdone it when you don't look like yourself. Like many women, I like hair extensions and makeup, but I too had to be delivered from not looking like myself. I went for years wearing contact lenses, to the point where Jay actually thought my eyes were a medium brown. As GOD was cleaning me up, HE began changing my mind, and I found myself loving me as I am more and more. Suddenly, I didn't want to wear colored contacts anymore, so on my next visit to the eye doctor, I requested clear contacts.

Suddenly, I didn't feel the need to wear makeup everywhere I went. I went bare-faced all around my town, and I was happy with me as I was. And for the extensions, I've worn braids for quite some time because I am growing my hair out, but there were many days where I considered just wearing my own hair. I would have never considered this a year prior to this incident. What was happening was that I was beginning to love the woman in the mirror just as GOD made her.

I know there will be some women who say they love themselves even though they cover themselves in all things fake. Nevertheless, I can truly testify and say that when you love yourself more, you'll begin to shed who you want to be to embrace who you are.

When that man meets you, he needs to get to know and see the real you. You don't want to present one woman to him, only for him to meet another one after the vows are said.

The Way You Carry Yourself

The way you carry yourself is not only important to your one-day-to-be husband; it is also important to your current and everlasting Husband, the LORD. Too many women carry themselves as single women instead of carrying themselves like wives. We walk by faith and not by sight. You shouldn't have to wait to see the manifestation of your husband before you start acting like a wife. That starts the day you ask GOD to send your husband to you.

It's not uncommon to go into a church and see many single women who drool over their pastors, leaders and other male members of the church. It's not uncommon to see a parade of flesh running around the church, hoping to be seen. Pay attention to the wives the most highly respected men have. These were the women who weren't half-dressed and sitting at the front of the church. They were oftentimes never seen until that man announced he would be getting married. That woman had been hidden; not by him, but by GOD. We often wonder where these women came from and how they nabbed such a great man when he had several beautiful women publicly parading themselves around him. The truth is, most men don't want women who are flamboyant or easy to catch. GOD created man to toil (or work for) whatever he wanted or needed. Anything a man doesn't toil for, he won't respect.

Instead of being the obvious and most logical choice of all the women any man could choose from, try being the one most women don't even notice. Women tend to notice women they perceive as their competition, but if you are not even a factor in their mind, you will become the one who stands out the most. If that man is your GOD-appointed husband, he will see you, recognize you and confirm you. Always remember how Esther behaved. Esther 2:12-17 (NIV) reads, "Before a young woman's turn came to go in to King Xerxes, she had to complete twelve months of beauty treatments prescribed for the women, six months with oil of myrrh and six with perfumes and cosmetics. And this is how she would go to the king: <u>Anything she wanted was given her to take with her from the harem to the king's palace.</u> In the evening she would go there and in the morning return to another part of the harem to the care of Shaashgaz, the king's eunuch who was in charge of the concubines. She would not return to the king unless he was pleased with her and summoned her by name.

When the turn came for Esther (the young woman Mordecai had adopted, the daughter of his uncle Abihail) to go to the king, <u>she asked for nothing</u> other than what Hegai, the king's eunuch who was in charge of the harem, suggested. <u>And Esther won the favor of everyone who saw her.</u> She was taken to King Xerxes in the royal residence in the tenth month, the month of Tebeth, in the seventh year of his reign. **Now the king was attracted to Esther more than to any of the other women**, and she won his favor and approval more than any of the other virgins. So he set a royal crown on her head and made her queen instead of Vashti."

Honestly, many women do too much to be seen, and clearly, this is what the other women did with King Xerxes. All you have to do is be the woman that you are with no additives. You don't have to be the loudest, prettiest or funniest woman in the crew. You don't have to wear the reddest lipstick or the longest weave. All you have to do is be hidden in the LORD, and the right man will find you there because he too will be searching the heart of GOD.

Stay hidden in the LORD. Don't run around telling everyone your relationship status, and don't lower your standards. GOD has a husband for you that will be far greater than the man you've envisioned yourself with. But to be found by him, you have to first be hidden. "Whoso findeth a wife findeth a good thing, and obtaineth favour of the LORD" (Proverbs 18:22).

Marrying Perception

Men often marry their perception of who a woman is, but they often divorce who she turns out to be.

As I was scrolling through Facebook, I went to the pages of a couple of well-known actresses because Facebook was suggesting them to me. I opened up one photo on each of the ladies' pages, and I began to read the comments. One thing I noticed were the comments from some of the men who were saying things like, "My kinda lady!" or "That's the kind of woman I need in my life!" One of the actresses often plays an aggressive woman who's usually fighting with her husband. I sat there and wondered how these men could say she (or the other women) was their type of lady. They didn't know any of these women personally. Sure, they were all beautiful women, but it was obvious that the men were speaking of the character roles these women had been playing in their shows and movies. They were in love with the characters, even though I'm sure they were attracted to the women as well, because again, they were all beautiful women.

But what if one of those women was to give one of those men a chance? What if she dated him, married him and had children with him? How long would he stay by her side? Let's say he's not in it for the money. Let's say he's a millionaire himself who happens to be in love with that woman's television character. In many cases, the divorce would be pending before the honeymoon was over. One man may marry a woman who plays an aggressive character, only to find that she's a sweet and passive person off screen. One man may marry a woman who plays a funny and witty character on the big screen, but he'd divorce her once he found her to be quiet, shy and predictable. Needless to say, if GOD sent her husband to her, that man would stick around because he's not marrying the character; he's marrying her.

When we date or court, we often play into a man's perception of us, especially if we believe we can handle the role. It's easy to pick up on what type of woman each man is looking for just by the things he says. By taking on these roles, we are essentially saying that we won't be ourselves anymore. We'll be that woman he's been searching for. The problem is, we simply cannot stop being who we are no matter how hard we try. That's why so many women have to "find themselves" once their marriages end. I don't care how strong of a woman you are, you will find yourself morphing into the woman your husband needs in his life. If you're not the right woman, you will abandon who you are to become who he wants. But the issue that will stand its ground will be the fact that you couldn't give up being you no matter how hard you tried. Sure, you'd pick up many personality traits and habits that he requires of his woman, but who you truly are will continue to radiate through who you are attempting to be, and that's when the fights will start.

Another perception men often marry is the belief that their new wife will mesh well with their friends. That's why men often introduce their women to the friends they want to keep around. They know that if a woman is against their friends, she'll eventually stand between them or give them an ultimatum. As women, we often pretend to like those friends for the sake of winning the man over. This is deception at its greatest. Please understand that a man's friends are a reflection of who he is, so if you do not like them, you don't really like him. You may be in love with who you think he can become one day, but you're not in love with the total picture of him. I've been guilty of this myself. In my first marriage, I really didn't like his most of friends because many of them were womanizers. In my second marriage, I really didn't meet his friends until after the marriage, and he had maybe two friends I was okay with. The rest of his friends were not the type of people I wanted sitting at my dining room table or even calling my house because they were culturally rooted and somewhat distant from their wives. They seemed to lead independent lives from their spouses. Some of his friends were even controlling towards him. In the end, what I discovered was that birds of a feather do truly flock together. It was the very things I disliked about their friends that would eventually be the elephants that sat on our marriages.

One of the lessons I took from those

experiences is to never pretend to be who you are not. Believe it or not, his friends matter more than you want them to. That's why it is very important to see who his friends are and watch for their fruit. If you end up marrying a man, you're going to have to deal with his friends visiting your house and influencing him and your children. If GOD sends the man to you, HE will send a wise man surrounded by wise friends. If the enemy sends a man to you, he will send a foolish man surrounded by even more foolish friends. Don't think for one second that you can marry the man, and then convince him to get rid of his friends. You'll only find yourself in pointless arguments where you'll become the bad guy, and his friends will be the good guys you're trying to attack.

Men tend to see a woman as she is or how she presents herself, and they marry the woman standing in front of them. Women tend to see the potential for change in a man, and they marry the man they believe he could become. This leads to a split down the marriage from the moment it starts, and in these cases, both parties are guilty.

The man is guilty because men often don't leave any room for change when it comes to their wives. They often expect us to remain the same for the rest of our lives. Many marriages have ended because a woman began to blossom into who GOD created her to be, and her husband didn't like who she was becoming. That's why you have to blossom first, and then GOD will let your husband find you...as you are. If you get a husband while in transition, you run the risk of losing him once you emerge from your cocoon.

The woman is guilty because she married an idea; nevertheless, she took a living and breathing person to the altar in place of that idea. Once the marriage began, the woman started introducing her new husband to her imagined husband. When he refused to be who she wanted in a husband, she began to punish him by arguing with him, withholding sex from him, and threatening to end the marriage. Of course, this is wicked behavior and is a surefire way to destroy a marriage.

Perception does not belong in marriage. You have to marry the actual person, flaws and all.

At the end of my second marriage, I found myself saying again and again, "I am who I am. I can't be anyone else." By this time, I'd not only realized who I was, but I realized that I loved me as I was. I can't be anyone else and I don't want to be anyone else. During that marriage, I would often say to Jay that he wanted a woman who would let his sister control her. A woman who didn't ask him any questions about the women who called him. A woman who'd let him be as selfish as he wanted to be, and a woman who would have absolutely no voice in her own home. I was really appalled at his response. He looked me in the eyes and said, "What's wrong with that?" It was then that I realized that not only had I made the mistake of marrying him, but there were many women who would make this very same mistake. They'd think they could love a man so much that he'd change for them. Jay often told me that when he married me, he thought I was submissive, sweet and obedient. Yes, he actually said he thought I was obedient because I often answered him with, "Okay, baby." That was his perception, but I was the total opposite. I'm submissive, but not passive; there is a difference. Had we not been led by perception, Jay and I would never have met each other at the altar.

Kill perception from the minute a man starts courting you by telling him who you are, how you are and what behaviors are deal breakers for you. In doing so, you won't waste his time, nor will he waste yours if he's not the GOD-appointed spouse for you. The problem with modern-day society is that most people date, but do not court. A man meets a woman who looks good to him, and he asks her on a date. All they are doing is spending time with one another, but in most cases, they aren't actually getting to know one another. From the minute he asks her on a date, the assumption begins that the two of them are in a relationship. After so many dates, the woman is expected to reward the man with sex. Of course, this is the world's way of doing things, but it has bled over into the church. In courting, however, the couple spends time getting to actually know one another, and trying to discern who they are to one another. In courting, you're not building a relationship with one another. You are learning to identify the role GOD has ordained you to play in the lives of each other. If GOD says the man is your husband, you then begin to build upon that foundation until the vows are said. A man can date a woman for ten years and still not marry her. But a man who courts a woman can marry a woman as soon as GOD confirms that she indeed is his own GOD-ordained wife. And we know that it doesn't take GOD long to confirm HIS plans for us.

The goal is to identify who the man is, and be confirmed by GOD. That's it. If you marry a man just because he looks and sounds like he could be a good catch, you'll eventually beg GOD to let you throw him back once you get a GOD'S-eye view of his heart. Oftentimes, GOD will let you stay there in that miserable marriage until you've picked up every lesson HE was trying to teach you when you were a single woman. Either way, you're going to get wisdom if you've asked for her. She'll either come in through the door you've opened for her, or she'll smash the windows of your heart and force you to look at slides of the truth.

Don't marry perception, and always make sure you ask GOD who every man is that enters your life. You'll save yourself from having a bunch of marriage tales that would make other women cringe.

Just Stop Waiting

This totally contradicts the title of the book, right? Why would I dare tell you to stop waiting? After all, you've almost perfected the art of waiting. You've been to tons of singles' seminars, read many books geared at single women, and you've waited a long time to be found by your husband. But that just might be the problem. You keep waiting, and you keep saying he's coming, when he's already there. Let me explain.

GOD is your husband. You know that already, but you say you're waiting on the man GOD has appointed you to as a wife. The truth is that if you are in the LORD and he is in the LORD, he's already found you. Right now, the two of you are only awaiting the manifestation of the promise. Look at it this way: Your husband is away doing some work for GOD right now. You are simply awaiting his return. "If ye abide in me, and my words abide in you, ye shall ask what ye will, and it shall be done unto you" (John 15:7).

The WORD is already established, and since it is already established, everything GOD said is already done. Faith makes you call what you've been praying for yours. Hope makes you call everything you've been waiting for over and over again. Once you ask for Mr. Right, you need to prepare for Mr. Right.

When Jay would go out of town, I would be excited when the time came for him to return. Even though I'd oftentimes be disappointed in him for not including me in his travel plans, I'd still be happy when the time came for him to come home. I knew he was coming back, so I would prepare our apartment for him. I'd buy new things, give the house a deeper clean and cook a hefty meal. I may have been pouting on the outside when he walked through the door, but I was smiling on the inside because my husband was home. At first, I used to wait for him, and I'd countdown the days until his return, and this was agonizing. As GOD began to mature me, I stopped waiting for him to come back, and I took every day as it was. Whenever he went out of town, I didn't wait for his comeback; I prepared for it. Imagine if ten women went into a church and five of them were carrying their suitcases. The other five were carrying their Bibles. The five women with the suitcases say they are moving into the church because they are waiting for JESUS to come back, so they want to be in the church when HE returns. The five with the Bible say they are living as the church, and they've got their Bibles with them because they are preparing for the coming back of the LORD. Which women do you think would get left behind? Those unprepared women who slept in an empty building, of course. We are the church; we are the temples of the HOLY SPIRIT.

A waiting woman often grows impatient and stumbles. A woman who's preparing often gets more patient as she learns to stand. Stop waiting and start preparing. Get your house in line, and ask the LORD to remove anything from your heart that keeps your husband from finding you.

His Story Repeats Itself

Every man has a story. When you meet a new guy, you don't know his story. All you know is whatever he tells you. If his story is full of scenes he knows will make you think twice about getting with him, he will give you a better version of his story or flat out tell you a lie.

One thing about getting into a relationship with a man is that his enemies will become your enemies. He may tell you stories of him being done wrong, and in your mind, the story will play out as if he is a noble and respectable character who could do no wrong. This person who betrayed him, on the other hand, will be a one-eyed monster whose day or recompense isn't coming fast enough. You'll stand with him against everyone who opposes him, but the problem with this is...if he isn't the right man, you may be standing up against the wrong people. You may find yourself dining with the villain and calling him a saint. Every man has a story, and it is very important that you know his story before you end up becoming a part of it.

Jay didn't have a lot of stories. He told me a few stories about a couple of friends who'd done him wrong, but he never really talked much about it. My first husband (we'll call him Mark) did have a lot of stories and a lot of enemies for me to consider. I listened to stories of betrayal, hurt and more. I found myself wondering how people could do such an innocent man so much wrong. Of course, that was at the beginning of our relationship and a few years into it. I was naïve because a woman in love will believe just about anything her husband tells her. Mark's enemies became my enemies. He even villanized the other women he'd been sleeping with. In his stories, he'd be an innocent man just trying to loan a hand to a co-worker or old friend, and that horrible woman tried to take advantage of his kindness. A couple of years into our marriage, however, I knew better. By the end of the marriage, based on what he'd taken me through, I was able to put those stories together using things he'd told me. I realized that he'd done the same thing to me as he'd done to the previous women. His story repeated itself. When I was blind and naïve, I was honored to be a part of his story until I realized I had the facts wrong.

When you marry a man, you are marrying his lies, his problems and all that is attached to him. His stories become your stories. The funny part is, anytime you marry an Ishmael, he's going to overload your ears with lies, and after a while, you'll be a walking vessel full of lies...but at least you have a man, right? That's how a lot of women think.

Whatever that man did to the women in his past, he is also going to do to you if he has not surrendered to GOD wholeheartedly. I'm not just talking about going to church every Sunday. That man has to be a new creature in CHRIST; otherwise, he will keep repeating his story until he runs out of characters. At the same time, if you aren't delivered from your past, you will keep repeating your story until you finally surrender to GOD wholeheartedly. It's not just that the man has to be changed for the relationship to work. You too have to be changed or else you'll keep playing the same role with a different cast of characters. Sure, you'll change a few things here and there, but ultimately, your story will remain the same.

The best place to get a man's story is oftentimes through his mother or sisters.

Women tend to be open books when it comes to their relatives. Of course, you should never be at his place with him unless there are people there, and GOD-fearing people coming with you for a public event such as a barbeque, bible study or garage sale. If you get the chance to meet his mother or sisters, don't be afraid to ask questions. You don't have to be blatant with your questions, however. You can ask them when you're alone with them or in a place where you know he won't be humiliated. A great way to get answers is to talk about funny things he's said or done in your presence, especially stories he's told you that you're unsure of. After that, look for body language, especially amongst his sister or sisters. The mother may try to lovingly cover her son's mishaps, but sisters aren't always the best at covering their brothers' strongmen. You'll find that many women will roll their eyes or stare at the man when they feel he's telling a lie.

If he keeps you away from his family, yet he frequents their house, that's a surefire sign that he's got some skeletons in his closet. Whatever you don't learn about him before getting with him, you will learn while with him.

I can't stress this enough: Don't go into a relationship and "see" or try to discern if the guy is the right guy. Take every man who attempts to court you before the altar of GOD immediately and ask GOD to reveal who they are and what is leading them.

His Height

As a short woman, I'm not too fond of short
men. I don't know why it's like that, but
most short women like average to tall men.
By the time a man is twenty years old, he's
finished growing. Some men can grow all
the way up until they are in their mid-
twenties, but ordinarily, once you are old
enough to marry, the man you're interested
in will have likely reached his maximum
height. Therefore, when you decide to
marry a man, you are taking him as he is;
flaws and all. Nevertheless, a man can
never grow too tall in the realm of the spirit
because he is created in the likeness of
GOD.

As a woman, you can and likely will mature
spiritually as well. You will learn so many
things about yourself as you go on through

life, encountering trial behind tribulation. Each challenge you face is an opportunity for you to grow some more. Every time you face a giant of a challenge, and you overcome it, you will find yourself being promoted in the realm of the spirit. As you grow in the LORD, the men you once found intriguing won't be so intriguing anymore. Men you see as giants today will be dwarfs tomorrow if you let the LORD continue to grow you up.

Pay attention to how you are when you work at a company. Every person who has a position higher than yours looks like a giant to you. Even if you don't see them as giants, you think they are making the megabucks. You'd love to earn what they are earning because their paychecks dwarf your paycheck. But once you got a better job, one where you were making more money than your old bosses, they suddenly don't look like giants anymore. For example, many teenagers and young adults work at fast food restaurants, and their managers are oftentimes thirty years of age or older. These young people look up to their managers; not because of their ages, but because of their wages. We are oftentimes the same way with men. We see men that we believe we can easily have, and then, there are those men who seem out of range to the average woman. It's easy to admire them from afar, thinking of how blessed their wives must be to have them. And for the ones who aren't married, it's easy to feel so dwarfed by them that you never take the time to consider that you could one day be the wife on their arms. It's all about perception, and how we perceive ourselves is oftentimes how we deceive ourselves.

But here's the amazing truth: GOD wants to grow you up so big that the large majority of those men whom you admire from afar will become dwarfs to you. Yes, including those celebrities you've drooled over. I know it may sound far-fetched, especially, if you've never imagined doing anything big with your life, or if you have never seen one of your family members do anything great with their lives. Nevertheless, GOD is always looking for an opportunity to glorify HIS Name amongst mankind, but the problem is there aren't too many people who open themselves up to be used by HIM at such a capacity. And that's why you should be busy in purpose right now, instead of sitting around and waiting to be found by your husband. If you're not in purpose, you are not prepared to be a wife. A wife is purposeful. She isn't just a woman; she is a creature of GOD. She isn't just an object that bears children; a woman is a fertile creature in every area of her life, and that's why we have to be careful who we let sow seeds in our lives.

One of the greatest obstacles that Christian women face today is that mountain called Patience. We see that great old mountain, and we want it to be removed and cast into the sea; nevertheless, GOD is calling us to wait on HIM. What we see as a mountain is actually a wall of protection for us. It is placed there to keep us from entering the right seasons at the wrong times. Can you imagine what would happen to a tomato if it was planted in the dead of winter? We are often so impatient, we try to find ways around that mountain because we want what we want when we want it. But no matter how hard we push, we can never make spring turn into fall. All we can do is wait the seasons out and dress properly for the weather we're in so we won't die from exposure. That's what happens when a woman uncovers herself for a man GOD has not called to cover her. That man exposes her to the realm of the demonic because he doesn't understand the type of covering she needs to get to where she's going. Instead, he enjoys the benefits and bonuses of being a married man without having the responsibilities of being a husband. Paying a bill doesn't make him worthy. The questions are: Can he minister to you when you need to be ministered to? Can he understand you when you enter a new level in the spirit? Can he lead you through the doors that GOD has opened for you? Make no mistake about it. If he hasn't walked through those doors himself, he can't lead you through them since he doesn't know the way.

A woman who waits eventually finds herself at a place where she's not only amazed by her new thinking, but she finds herself disgusted by her old thinking patterns. Suddenly, those decisions she made in 2012 aren't the same decisions she'd make in 2013 because in those twelve months, she's come a long way. Think about that one guy you wanted so much when you were in elementary, junior or high school. He was so handsome to you, and you imagined him holding your hands and sharing an ice cream sundae with you. But there was a problem. You were just an average girl whose parent's didn't earn much money. His parents were well off, on the other hand, so he was always in a relationship with one of the women who had well-to-do parents. Even though you thought he was cute, you said nothing to him. You simply admired him from afar, and he simply didn't notice you at all. One day, you grew up and filled out to be a beautiful woman and you ran into him. He's no longer that beautiful hunk of a man you once had trouble keeping your eyes off of. He's now well beneath your standards, and suddenly, he's interested in you. After turning him down, you walk away wondering how you could have ever had a crush on him. Can you believe that this scenario can actually

happen in a marriage? Let me elaborate.
Let's say you meet a man who you see as a
giant. He seems to be more knowledgeable
than you; he has a better paying job, and
he's handsome. To you, he's a catch, so you
set out to have him. Now, he's your
husband and he's not so great of a catch
anymore because you've grown, and he
hasn't. Over the course of your marriage,
you started operating in your purpose and
GOD began to ascend you up the spiritual
ranks. Your husband, on the other hand, is
stagnant and intimidated by you. Your
relationship was great when you
worshipped him with your eyes and
admired his every move. He basked in all
the praise you gave him, but nowadays,
you're too busy being who you really are,
and he's no longer interested in you. All the
same, you're no longer fascinated by him.
At one point, you saw him as a giant, but
now, you see him as a fallen giant. He goes
off to find a new woman who sees the hero

in him, while you're busy in purpose.
Before you know it, you're in divorce court,
and he wants half of what you've earned.
After all, he needs money to rescue that
new woman he's trying to impress. Sounds
outlandish, right? This happens more than
we know. One thing about us women is we
are ashamed of having men who don't add
to us. We'll come home and push our
husbands, but those loving nudges we give
them may feel like fist strikes to men who
feel as if they've been castrated by their
wives' success.

The point is: You have NO idea how tall GOD
has called you to grow, and because you
don't know this, you have no idea how tall
your GOD-ordained husband will be. It's
easy to go out and get with a short guy who
meets you eye-to-eye right now, but what
happens tomorrow if he's reached his
maximum height and you continue to grow?
It's simple. He won't be able to properly

cover you, and because of this, you'll lose respect for him. Men often lose their attraction to women who dwarf them, and women often lose respect for the men who look up to them. And this is why you should build, build and build some more until GOD tells you to stop. You want to meet the husband who can cover you twenty-five years from now, not just a man who can uncover you today and meet you in your right-now understanding. Always remember that you were designed to grow. If you stay in the WORD of GOD, you are going to grow. You just don't know how tall you'll be in the realm of the spirit until you get there.

Again, some of the men who are intimidating to you today won't be so intimidating in the future. Don't look at a man's height right now; focus on who you are in the LORD so you'll grow up in the loving arms of your FATHER. When the man

GOD has for you comes along, he will be tall enough to reach you, cover you and he'll be knowledgeable enough to maintain your respect.

Lying to Yourself

Before I met Jay, I'd started seeing a man we'll call Larry. Larry was older than me by about thirteen years, but I was attracted to his drive and intelligence. He was making six figures a year and seemed to have his life in order. I thought an older guy would be a better fit for me because I was settled and ready to settle down. I didn't want any more adulterers; I wanted a man who was "about his business", but at that time, I didn't understand that I needed the man who was "about my FATHER'S business." Of course, I was attracted to Larry physically and that's how he ended up with my phone number, but the main attraction I had with him was his intelligence. I've always been attracted to intelligent men, and I was fascinated with his knowledge of computers, computer language and all-things-computers. He seemed to have his head on straight, and he came off as a man who had no time for games.

My accountability partner called me one day, and we began to talk about Larry and men in general. She asked me that question I'd hoped she wouldn't ask me. She asked, "Tiff, have you prayed about Larry, yet?" I hesitated. I hadn't asked GOD about Larry because I pretty much knew the answer. He was definitely not Mr. Right, but I liked him, so I wanted to keep him around for a bit. After I answered her, she responded, "Tiff, you already know our prayer. Ask GOD that if Larry isn't the man HE has for you to drive him away from you." I felt myself becoming agitated with her, even though I knew she was telling the truth. But the enemy came in, countered her words, and said to me, "Look at all those Ishmaels she dated, and now she has the nerves to come and try to end your relationship. She wouldn't let you come between her and her friends." Rather than accepting the truth, I began to embrace the lies. Larry was definitely not Mr. Right, and I knew this, but he did make for a decent Mr. Right Now. Howbeit, I couldn't get around the truth, no matter how hard I tried. Even though I was a little irritated with my friend, I agreed to say the prayer and let GOD drive Larry away if needed.

Not long after praying that prayer, I had a conversation with Larry that would change my mind about him.

One day, when speaking with Larry, I asked him what the longest relationship he'd ever had was, and he said three years. This was baffling to me. I was still in my twenties, and I'd been in longer relationships than that, and here he was in his forties and had never held a relationship down for more than three years. That immediately sent up a red flag with me. I also brought up my tumultuous relationship with Mark, and how he used to fight me. I wanted to get Larry's take on it. I expected him to say in his deep, masculine voice, "That's a coward! Any man who hits a woman is a coward, and I wish he'd step to me!" That would have been the answer I was looking for, but instead, he began to tell me about a tumultuous relationship he was once a part of. In Larry's story, a woman he was dating was visiting his mother's house with him one day, and the two of them began to argue. She became disrespectful in his mother's house and began to hit him. His mother demanded that they go outside, and once outside, he'd slammed her to the ground, mounted her and began force-feeding her grass. That was it. I'd just come out of a physically violent relationship, and I definitely didn't want a man who'd shove grass down my throat. Before I could end the call, Larry kept asking me about a clicking sound on the line. This had been happening for a few days by then, and I suspect it may have just been crossed signals or a bad signal. Nevertheless, I could tell that Larry thought it was something else. He asked me if I was recording our calls, which was a ridiculous question. Why would he think I'd be recording our calls? It was obvious to me that Larry was paranoid about something, and every time he'd hear the clicking noise, he'd get off the phone with me. After that conversation, Larry and I stopped calling one another. GOD had answered my prayer; Larry was definitely Mr. Wrong.

There were other warning signs there. As a matter of fact, when I look back, there were obvious signs in all of those relationships, but I chose to ignore them and lie to myself. Now, when ministering to women, I recognize that lying spirit the minute a woman tries to justify standing by her Ishmael. Remembering how stubborn and unyielding I was helps me to remain patient with women who are at those places I once found myself in. Ministering to a woman who is stubbornly grounded in a soul tie is like trying to uproot a tree with a fork. She's often unmoving and will not receive the truth until she is forced to look at it.

We often lie to ourselves when we don't want to believe that the man we're interested in is not the one for us. We've already made plans for him in our hearts, and we've already drowned our imaginations with thoughts of him in our futures. We've already seen what we believe our children will look like. We've already started window shopping for our homes, and we've already told ourselves that he is Mr. Right or we'll teach him how to be Mr. Right. Once we've marinated our hearts in lies, we become stubborn and unyielding. When trying to help a woman come out of a soul tie, there is pretty much nothing you can do but pray for her.

One thing about lies is that they attract
more lies. In order to believe the lies you've
told yourself and the lies your beau has told
you, you must first reject the truth. Once
lies come in, you have to keep telling
yourself more lies as each lie you've
believed starts to peel away, revealing the
truth you've tried to bury. For every lie
you've told or believed, you will have to tell
a lifetime of lies to cover it up and keep it
covered. At the same time, your
relationship will be just as unstable as the
lies it's built on.

Building a Solid Foundation

When I first met Jay, I had a hip hop website where I promoted artists and half-dressed models. Even though I was a Christian woman, I was obviously still a baby. The LORD had told me that I would build a website, but being a baby Christian, I went and built a hip hop site. Jay was attracted to the sin in me, but what he didn't understand was the woman who talked about GOD all the time. Because I was willing to sin against GOD back then, he didn't take my walk in CHRIST seriously. I did take it seriously, but I just didn't know how to live a righteous life. I knew how to sin, and that was that.

The foundation of my relationship with Jay was sin. After all, my divorce wasn't finalized, so our relationship ended up being an adulterous one. I was promoting music that went against the WORD of GOD, and I was unrepentant. Sure, I felt bad about sinning, but feeling bad and being repentant aren't the same. I had the same attitude as many women who enter relationships and begin to sin against the LORD. I felt like I was sinning towards righteousness. Jay needed sin to be reassured that I was serious about our relationship. Honestly, Satan always requires a sin offering, and that's why any man sent by Satan will require a sin offering. He may not ask for it by name, but he will definitely lead or drag you towards sin. I didn't realize it then, but Jay and I were building a foundation together; one that would be shaken by the truth, and destroyed by lies.

Now that I'm older and wiser, I understand where I went wrong with both Jay and Mark. The issue wasn't that the men betrayed me and deserved the worst to happen to them. The issue was that I was a woman of GOD who was still a baby in CHRIST when I entered those relationships. Had I been more WORD rooted, I would have known better. That's why it is NEVER a good idea to enter a relationship when you aren't spiritually mature. If you do, you could end up with a religious devil who leads you in false doctrine and not in the LORD. Or you could end up with an abusive man, a womanizer, an unforgiving man or just a man who does not love you. Some men do marry women they don't love because they think they love these women. They experience romantic obsession and confuse it with love. Some men are only attracted to the anointing on the women they are courting. Some men are only attracted to a woman's intelligence or profession, and they end up in what I like to refer to as corporate relationships. Some men are only attracted to the physique of the women they are courting. Whatever it is, GOD knows, and that's why you need to get HIS approval before entering any courtship. You don't want to end up in relationships where love isn't present, but expectation is. You don't want to end up in relationships where GOD isn't present, but Satan is. It is very important to build a solid foundation on the WORD and continue building from there. Any man who tries to build on any other foundation except the WORD is clearly an Ishmael. It is better to end your association with him before it turns into a relationship and, eventually, a soul tie.

From the minute you meet Mr. Right, you should both already have an established foundation on CHRIST. What you are doing is bringing your foundations together as one. From the minute you meet Mr. Wrong, you should be so established in the WORD that your refusal to sin should repel him.

You are going to meet some Mr. Wrongs. That's a given, but if you do what GOD tells you to do, you won't end up marrying any man that's not GOD-approved. At the same time, when you meet a Mr. Wrong, you will find that you were oftentimes in the wrong. Maybe you were at a party that you knew you weren't supposed to go to. Maybe you were hanging out with some friends that GOD told you to let go of. Maybe you were walking in pride and forgot to humble yourself.

Also be aware that Mr. Wrong will pretend to be Mr. Right if he can figure out the type of man you're waiting for. He will even attempt to build a Christian foundation with you, but he won't be able to hide his desire to sin and lead you into sin for too long. Once you realize that he's leading you away from GOD, disassociate yourself from him immediately and continue to wait in GOD and on GOD for your husband. Any other man is just applying to be your ex-husband or sex-husband.

Unfortunately, many Christian women have testimonies like mine. They met a man who they weren't sure of, and in many cases, they saw the signs that he wasn't the right one. But they'd been waiting and waiting, and finally, when some guy came along who looked like he'd make a decent husband, they bit the bait. Satan fished them right on out of the truth and tossed them into a sea of confusion; one where he would toy with them and agonize them for years on end.

Midway through my relationship with Jay, I began to cry out to GOD a lot. I thought that part of my punishment for being so stubborn was that HE would leave me with Jay for the rest of my life. Sure, many people will say that I could have easily gotten up and walked away at any time, but walking away is never as easy as it sounds.

At the same time, I'd made such a huge mistake in how I handled my divorce with Mark that I was determined to clearly hear from GOD before I made my move with Jay. I knew I'd likely be married again one day, and this time, I wanted to do things GOD'S way. I was determined to hear from Heaven before I walked away, so I focused on the good in Jay. He was a quiet man who didn't like to argue. He often told me that divorce was not an option. In his culture, they didn't believe in divorce, and I felt somewhat reassured by those words. I wanted to believe that Jay would change and become the man of GOD that I so desired. As the years passed, I began to hunger for that Godly relationship that a husband and wife has. Here I was married, but I still felt alone. As GOD sent more and more single women for me to minister to, I found myself feeling like a public spectacle of what you're not supposed to do. I felt like I was on exhibit in a museum, and women would come by to gawk at the mess I'd made of my life. I wanted to make sure no woman ended up with my testimony, so I unashamedly shared my story with them, often going into another room so Jay wouldn't hear me. Most of the time, he'd be on his phone with Mara anyway, so I'd excuse myself while I told my story to yet another woman. In a way, I began to look at them as free women. They still had the chance to do things GOD'S way and end up with their GOD-ordained husbands, and here I was feeling stuck in a loveless marriage. I felt like it was too late for me, but they could at least save themselves. But in the midst of thinking like that, GOD continued to speak to my heart, and HE said to me that the foundation of my marriage was being tested and destroyed. In order for our marriage to survive, we would have to rebuild our marriage on a Godly foundation. HE told me that most marriages don't survive the destruction of its ungodly foundation, but I stood in there. I told GOD that either Jay was to change or I didn't want the marriage at all. As the foundation began to crumble, I found myself losing more and more of my respect for Jay because I didn't see him trying to rebuild or fix anything. He'd sit in his favorite spot and stare at his computer screen day in and day out. He'd pick up his phone and call his family and friends, but he wouldn't talk to me too much, even though I was sitting a few feet from him. As the foundation began to crumble, Jay found himself losing interest in me all the more. There was a time when I'd fight hard to keep our marriage together, but all of a sudden, I wasn't fighting anymore. He totally depended on me to save our marriage. He didn't like confrontation and he definitely hated any talks about problems in our marriage. He thought the answer to every problem was sex. Why? Because one of the foundations of our marriage was sex. Sex was a tool I'd used to get him, so sex was needed in order for me to keep him.

What's the point of all this? The very foundation that you build your relationship on is going to be tested. Ask any married couple, and they will tell you about the tests that challenged their marriages. Ask any divorced couple, and they will tell you about the tests that destroyed their marriages. Ask any separated couple, and they will tell you about the tests that divided them. Divorce rates are so high because most couples build their marriages on the wrong foundations. If CHRIST is your foundation, how can you go wrong except one of you first abandons the LORD? Make sure that any man who wants your attention first be attentive to the WORD of GOD. If you know more WORD than he does, you may want to wait for him to get more WORD in him so he can properly lead you; otherwise, the foundation of your marriage may be good, but the covering (husband) isn't built up enough to cover just yet. It is possible to marry the right man in the wrong season, and he may end up being worse than the wrong man in any season. Please don't become impatient and try to fill your voids with a relationship. Let GOD set you up with the right man, and let GOD lead you, and it is then and only then that you'll be able to better understand why GOD has to be the head of your life and the foundation of your marriage.

The Power of Your Testimony

For a long time, I was ashamed of my testimony. I didn't mind sharing it with the women I'd personally spoken with, but to go public with it was hard. I knew that going public meant dealing with public perception, judgment, ridicule and worse of them all, pity. But here's what I learned:

- Your testimony is not for you; it's for others. You are just the vessel who delivers it. Don't get caught up in your own reflection. Think of those people out there who need to hear your story.
- Anytime you worry about public perception, you need to uproot pride. Pride always makes you worry more about yourself than others.
- There are different types of people on the earth. Some of them want to be

delivered, some of them do not want to be delivered, and others are gossipers. A gossiper's Satanic assignment is to silence one's testimony. If you withhold your testimony because of the gossipers, you have given them the power to shut you up. At the same time, you become a broken vessel because you're not delivering the good news to those who want to be delivered.

- Telling your story not only helps others, but it helps you to not repeat it.

Revelation 12:11: "And they overcame him by the blood of the Lamb, and by the word of their testimony; and they loved not their lives unto the death."

Many women aren't found by their GOD-appointed husbands because they haven't yet overcome the things that have happened to them. Because they have kept their stories dammed up, they began to swell with pride and walk in a straight line to keep others from noticing that they are different from them. You see, we live in a society that fears what it does not understand and what it cannot control; therefore, many of us pretend to be "normal" and we pretend to be "controllable," all the while, who we are is screaming to come out. I am no longer ashamed of my testimony. As a matter of fact, I'm blessed to have it because not only did I learn from it, but it blessed me with the opportunities to help others.

I remember ministering a girl one day who was just exiting an abusive relationship. Her husband had not only been beating on her, he'd been biting her, raping her and even attacked her while she was pregnant with their son. After speaking with her for the first time, she said to me that other ministers had called her, but she could not receive anything from them. She said that these women were in great marriages and they'd boasted that their husbands had never hit them. She felt that they couldn't understand her, but she was comfortable with me because I'd been in an abusive marriage before. I could relate to her. It was during that time that I realized why GOD didn't send perfect people out to minister to imperfect people. Women who used to be prostitutes can easily go out and minister to women who are prostitutes because those who are not delivered won't feel judged by them. Men who were once drug addicted can easily minister to men who are drug addicted, because the addicts would know that the former addicts understand where they are and how to get them out. But the problem is, the enemy has convinced so many people to be silent victims rather than people who shout their victories from the rooftops. In staying silent, they don't overcome. Instead, they continue to repeat the cycles that they've learned to live in, eventually believing that there is no hope for them.

What's your story and why aren't you sharing it with a woman who could be blessed by it? When I began to tell women about my relationship with Jay, I began to overcome the things he'd done and was doing...and I was still married to him! Suddenly, the pain began to fade and I saw Jay as the broken soul he was. I began to feel more compassion for him, and I began to pray for him more. Once our marriage ended, I continued to tell my story, finally coming out publicly with it. The response was amazing. There are so many women and men who've suffered similar hurts, and many of them are ashamed of their testimonies. They thanked me for being bold enough to share my story with the world, but what they didn't know was that in sharing it, I felt even more freed. That's when I understood what Revelation 12:11 meant. "And they overcame him by the blood of the Lamb, and by the word of their testimony; and they loved not their lives unto the death."

My challenge to you is to get out and visit some shelters, prisons and anyplace broken women frequent. Share your testimony with them, and watch yourself get set free. Before you do, however, make sure you:

- **Forgive those who have hurt you.** You don't want to go there with the intent to testify, only to find yourself ranting. I remember the LORD led me to share my story with an older woman once. We were supposed to be talking about business, but I felt led to share my story with her. After I did, she began to tell me about what her ex-husband did to her. He'd left her for another woman, and I could tell she was still angry with him for that. She told me that she knew he would get it all back and that his marriage to his current wife would not last. Just by her words, I thought their breakup had been recent and the current woman was the old mistress, but I was taken aback when she told me that they'd been broken up for more than a decade. At the same time, the current wife he had was not the same woman who'd helped destroy their marriage. I began to intercede for that man's marriage almost immediately. She'd been single for more than a decade because she hadn't forgiven the man who'd hurt her back then. That man moved on, and had she done the same, she could have been happily married by then. Forgive!

- **Take accountability for your own wrong.** In doing so, you release those who have done you wrong because you'll understand that your choice to be with them set in motion everything that happened to you. I forgive Jay and Mark, and I will always love them both with sisterly love. They weren't the worst of the worst. They were just lost souls that I thought I could save. All the same, I wasn't perfect or completely innocent in those marriages either. I was contentious (with Mark), prideful (with Jay), and I refused to submit to either one of them. Later on in my marriage to Jay, GOD told me to submit to him, but learn the difference between Jay and the spirit that was in operation within him. I listened and submitted to Jay when he was speaking, but when he started talking crazy...I knew I wasn't talking with my husband.

- **Don't operate in false humility.**

Really take accountability for what you've done wrong and really forgive the men. I've listened to people who operated in false humility, and that is brought on by a haughty spirit. False humility doesn't help anyone. In looking at you and hearing you speak, they'll know that you're still bound by those relationships, and they may feel that there is no hope for them after all.

- **Share your story ONLY for the purpose of testifying.** Don't share it to humiliate the people who've hurt you. For a long time, I didn't share my stories about Mark because I wanted to protect him. I don't see him or Jay as men who've hurt me because I've healed from those hurts. I see them as my ex-husbands, but more than that, I see them as souls who I will always wish the best for. While Jay and I were together, I began to share my stories more because I saw a need with the women of GOD, and I knew that GOD wanted me to help them. To do that, I had to tell my story.

- Commit to GOD that you will never sin against HIM with your body again. Sure, we're not perfect, but we can make decisions ahead of time to keep us from fornicating. If you make a list of things that you won't do and how you will approach each situation with men, and you lay it at the altar, you are more likely to remain celibate until marriage. Once we commit to GOD not to do something, we will work harder to make sure we don't do it.

Closing Doors

Every night before bed, I check all of my doors to make sure that they are locked. Every now and again, I'll check the sliding door to my patio to make sure it's also locked. Since I never go out on my patio, I automatically assume it's locked everyday; nevertheless, I still check it from time to time.

A few days ago, I dreamed I was suspicious that someone may have been coming in and out of my patio, so I went to check the door. Even in my dream, I knew that I never went out that door, so there was no reason for it to be unlocked. When I pushed the handle on the door, the door opened easily. I stood there, afraid, and then I started trying to close and lock the door. No matter what I did, the door didn't seem to want to lock. After a few tries, I woke up.

Revelation:

Many of us are constantly checking doors in the realm of the spirit, trying to make sure that they are all closed, but there are often one or more doors that we don't check often. It is those doors that allow the enemy access to us, and if we were to ever check those doors, we'd find them open. What doors are they?

- **Past relationships**
- **Current relationships**
- **Friendships**
- **Family relationships**
- **Unforgiveness**
- **Debt or indebted thinking**
- **Fear**

It is our relationships with people that hinder us from relationships with other people. If you refuse to close a door, you are in the same telling GOD that you don't want HIM to open any new doors for you because you intend to stay behind.

304

But let's talk about debt and indebted thinking. Of course we know what debt is. Most of us even know that having debt is wrong because it places us in bondage to other human beings, when CHRIST has set us free. So, first and foremost, you need to work on the debt you have and clear your name; otherwise, you enslave the man who's coming to marry you. Many women sit and wait for a man to come along and clean up their debt, but they end up attracting men who are like themselves; men who are also in debt. Do not see a man as your way out. Work on yourself and your debt while you are still single so you will be a blessing when GOD sends your husband.

As far as indebted thinking, there are many women who feel they owe someone something because that person did something for them. It's similar to unforgiveness because in unforgiveness, you feel someone owes something to you. But with indebted thinking, you feel you owe something to someone. Oftentimes, we take on this mindset when a friend or family member does something for us that we are truly thankful for. They went out of their way to help us, and many of us will spend the rest of our lives trying to pay them back over and over again. This is sinful thinking because in feeling indebted to someone, you are denying yourself the freedom CHRIST has paid the price for.

Romans 13:8: Owe no man any thing, but to love one another: for he that loveth another hath fulfilled the law.

I've seen this happen a lot in friendships, where one woman helped a friend out when she was in need. The friend who was helped then refuses to do anything she feels may offend the woman who helped her. That includes serving the LORD with her whole heart or staying in a relationship that her friend does not approve of. Believe it or not, a large number of women feel indebted to other women and men. At the same time, there are actually women (and men) out there who do things for others just so they will feel indebted to them. They are slave masters who have learned how to acquire inexpensive slaves. If someone feels you owe them something based on something they did for you, they are not a friend; they are a slave master. Pay them back whatever you took from them so they don't become a stumbling block to you.

Matthew 5:23-26: Therefore if thou bring thy gift to the altar, and there rememberest that thy brother hath ought against thee; Leave there thy gift before the altar, and go thy way; first be reconciled to thy brother, and then come and offer thy gift. Agree with thine adversary quickly, whiles thou art in the way with him; lest at any time the adversary deliver thee to the judge, and the judge deliver thee to the officer, and thou be cast into prison. Verily I say unto thee, Thou shalt by no means come out thence, till thou hast paid the uttermost farthing.

Proverbs 6:1-5: My son, if thou be surety for thy friend, if thou hast stricken thy hand with a stranger, Thou art snared with the words of thy mouth, thou art taken with the words of thy mouth. Do this now, my son, and deliver thyself, when thou art come into the hand of thy friend; go, humble thyself, and make sure thy friend.
Give not sleep to thine eyes, nor slumber to thine eyelids. Deliver thyself as a roe from the hand of the hunter, and as a bird from the hand of the fowler.

The problem with being indebted to someone is that you are operating as the property of that person. In doing so, you are not free to marry anyone. Sometimes

the very thing that keeps your husband
from finding you is something as slight as
you already being taken...only as a slave.
Owe your friends nothing but to love them,
and if you discern that they feel entitled to
you or as if you owe them something, you
need to deliver yourself from them. Speak
with them, and if they refuse to change
their view of you and their ways towards
you, you will need to distance yourself from
them. Good examples of such friends
include, but are not limited to:

- Friends who want to know your every
  move.
- Friends who are offended if you don't
  tell them certain personal details
  about your life, conversations and
  choices.
- Friends who feel that any man who
  courts you has to have their approval
  before continuing with the courtship.
- Friends who feel that any man who
  courts or marries you should come

second to them because they've been around longer.

- Friends who feel comfortable enough to disrespect your male friend.
- Friends who are offended when you don't answer your phone or don't answer your phone fast enough.
- Friends who get offended if you tell them no for any reason.
- Friends who become offended when you get off the phone with them to talk to your male friend or anyone for that matter.

Please note that such characters are not friends. Again, they are slave masters, and to them, you are their personal property. Such relationships can and do keep many women from being found by their GOD-ordained husbands.

Ask GOD to show you any open doors in your life that HE has not opened. Once you see those open doors, repent and ask the

LORD to close them. You'd be amazed at how much faster your husband will find you, and how things will begin to fall into place in your life once those demonic access doors are closed.

Unplugged

Have you ever had one of those days where you knew you had a lot to do, but you just didn't feel like doing anything? On those days, you felt heavy, depressed and you wanted to stuff your face with junk food and watch television. You weren't necessarily going through a hormonal change, it was just one of those days where you felt powerless. Days like that are days when we welcome the sound of the rain, but the sight of sunshine can be depressing because we know we're missing out on a beautiful day to wallow in whatever we're feeling. Days like that feel hopeless, but a little cry seems to do a little good for the soul. If you've had a day like that, relax. You're a woman.

But what's going on during those days when

we feel like throwing in the towel and retreating back to the life we've once known? It's simple. Sometimes, something we said, listened to or believed has caused us to unplug our faith from GOD. GOD is the source of our power, but our faith plugs us in to HIM, and it is through our faith that we access every blessing HE has for us. It's amazing how the soul knows when it's out of line. It's also amazing how we tend to feed the very thing that's weighing us down in times of hardship: our flesh. When the flesh rises up against you, you should always tear it down with a fast.

In your time spent waiting or preparing for Mr. Right, you will be attacked by the enemy. His goal is to cause you to doubt GOD. In doubting GOD, you evict much of the knowledge that's stored up in your heart, and this gives the enemy room to bring lies in. His plan is to get you to doubt GOD and believe him. He wants to cause you to abort GOD'S plan for you. He wants to cause you to look back at a time when you lived comfortably in ignorance, and he'll make that time look like it was the best time of your life. He'll then let you turn around to look towards your future, and all you will see is a blank slate. You have your plans, you have your dreams, and you have GOD'S WORD, but the mind can't really wrap itself around events that haven't happened yet. It's possible to relive the past, but it's impossible to pre-live the future.

Please know this: The enemy is always seeking to unplug you from GOD. He does not want to see you living in the blessings GOD has stored up for you. He wants to see you living in the very misery he's damned to. The enemy hates marriage with an undying passion because the coming together of two believers is too powerful of a union for him. "Again I say unto you, That if two of you shall agree on earth as touching any thing that they shall ask, it shall be done for them of my Father which is in heaven. For where two or three are gathered together in my name, there am I in the midst of them" (Matthew 18:19-20). Anytime two people come together in the Name of the LORD, they invite GOD in their midst. At the same time, if they agree and ask anything in the Name of the LORD, nothing will be withheld from them.

So, how does the enemy fight the marriage union? It's simple. Send the wrong man to each woman of GOD during her growth stages. Send a man to her when she's not yet ready to be crowned as a wife, and make sure that he looks like a catch. Create a void in that woman by getting her to think that she needs a man in certain areas of her life. That way, she rejects GOD in those areas. If he can get a believing woman with an unbelieving man, the two of them will rarely agree, and this brings dissension or wrath into the marriage. Just as GOD said that if we are gathered together in HIS Name, HE is in the midst, we must also remember that GOD said not to let the sun go down on our wrath, neither give place unto the devil. Therefore, in our matrimonial dealings with one another, we either invite GOD in or we invite the enemy. The devil's goal is to get an invitation into your life through your marriage. After he's done this, he'll use that marriage against you. He knows how hard you'll love your husband. He knows that you can't imagine life without your husband. He even knows that some women will take their lives because of their husbands. He wants to make your life a living hell, and many women have given him the license to do so by marrying his sons.

Anytime you marry the wrong man, that man will do everything in his power to unplug you from your faith. There will be good days; days where he encourages you in the faith and seems to love you unconditionally. Then there will be bad days; days when he discourages you and drags you far from your faith by your heart. Please understand that the enemy knows you're a woman. He knows how you're built. He knows how you're designed, and he uses that very design against you. "There is difference also between a wife and a virgin. The unmarried woman careth for the things of the Lord, that she may be holy both in body and in spirit: but she that is married careth for the things of the world, how she may please her husband" (1 Corinthians 7:34). When a woman is married, her heart will long for her husband, even while he's in the same house with her. A man can live with you and still be distant. A wife will seek to please her husband, and when she's neglected or rejected, she will feel broken and become distracted by her own pain. This causes her to unplug from her faith and seek ways to mend her marriage. An unplugged wife is emotional because she's no longer driven by faith; she is being driven to the brinks of insanity by fear. Marrying the wrong man will always prove to be a disaster that causes a woman to lament for her husband. Even when married to the wrong man, your heart will still cry out for your GOD-ordained husband, but your soul will cry out for the man you've married.

Stay plugged into the LORD at all times, and when you feel yourself slipping away, power up on the WORD of GOD. Just as GOD has plans for you, the enemy has plans for you, but it is your faith or your lack thereof that will determine whose plans take root in your life. One of the most undetected issues with believing women is that they tend to plug into the wrong men because they've unplugged from GOD somewhere in their lives, minds or heart. Faith will take you the full distance in HIM, but the enemy is going to shake your faith, try your faith and do whatever he can to destroy your faith. You need a daily helping of the WORD and an unyielding determination to get you to where GOD has appointed you to go. Stay plugged into the LORD by staying tuned up with HIS WORD. Store HIS WORD in your heart, and let nothing move you from GOD. If you are powered up by GOD, only a powerful man in GOD will be able to touch you and not be destroyed. A woman who stays in the LORD is like the Ark of the Covenant. She has the glory of GOD radiating from her, and anyone who touches her without HIS permission will fall by the wayside.

Thinking Like a Wife

Anytime I'm out at the store or in a public place, I can almost always look at a woman and tell if she's married or not. If I talk with a woman, I can likely discern whether she's married or not. How so? Married women tend to carry themselves differently than single women. Nevertheless, single women who are Godly and preparing for their husbands tend to carry themselves like wives.

Single women tend to wear more fitted clothes and add a little sway to their hips when they walk. Single women tend to talk louder and it's hard for them to stay focused. Instead, they look at almost everyone who passes them by...especially men. Single women tend to involve themselves in family drama and gossip more than married women. Because of these behaviors, many single women remain single.

There are many women in their fifties and sixties who are still waiting for their GOD-appointed husbands to come. Why is this? Oftentimes, it's a mindset they have that's keeping him away. Sometimes, it's just not their season to be found. One thing I've witnessed with single women (young and old) who are held back because of their mindsets is that they tend to overdo it with the clothing, hair and makeup. Too many women think it's all about dressing up the body, when in truth, they should have been dressing up their minds. I always tell people that I can go outside at any given time and come home with a new boyfriend. Why is that? I'm a woman. There are plenty of men looking for women. Nevertheless, to be found by Mr. Right, I would have to stay hidden in the LORD.

Anytime you spend too much money on your outer appearance, you are investing in carnal men. The thing about your GOD-ordained husband is that he is looking for his help meet, his partner in life, the woman he'll spend his life with. Carnal-minded men, however, are looking for beautiful, shapely women to show off to their friends. Sure, almost every man wants to be attracted to his wife physically, but a wise man will be attracted to her physically, mentally and spiritually. Ask any man this question: Which would you rather have? An extremely beautiful woman who you have absolutely nothing in common with, or an average looking woman who you have a lot in common with? Most men will opt for the average looking woman. Why so? Beauty is just a bonus with most men. It's not the deal-maker.

Nevertheless, most women spend too much money trying to be glamorous, single women, and they end up growing old and asking their grandchildren to call them "Glam-ma" instead of Grandma.

You'll notice that when most married women are out and about, they aren't trying to be seen. Instead, they may wear basic clothing, no makeup and have their hair swept back in a ponytail. If they're on their cell phones talking, you'll notice that they keep their voices down, and when they walk through the store, they aren't looking at everyone who passes them by. They stay focused because what they've come to the store to get is likely on a shelf, and it's not moving. Many single women, however, want to be ready whenever Mr. Right finds them, so their eyes are all over the place.

Anytime you see a single woman who isn't acting like a single woman, watch her. It won't be long before she's married. Most wise men aren't into a woman wearing an extra long wig, fake eyelashes, extra long nails, tons of makeup and fitted jeans. A carnal-minded man will see a woman like that and know she's on the market.

Sure, you want to be found by your husband, but make sure you don't walk around advertising yourself to a bunch of men who want to see what you look like unwrapped. Every man isn't marriage material, and every man isn't looking to be married. Many men simply want a woman they can call their "girlfriend" or "friend-with-benefits", but not a wife. In your choosing, you will never be able to pick out the best man for yourself. You have to let GOD do it. What's amazing is that the husband GOD has for you will probably find you on a bad hair day wearing a t-shirt and jogging pants, and you'll still be the only woman he notices. Please understand that he's looking for a life-partner, and any man who is looking for his wife will search the heart of a woman, rather than looking at how much makeup she's put on or how many clothes she's taken off.

10 Tips on Thinking Like a Wife

1. Less is always more. Don't decorate yourself like an Easter egg. Remember, GOD knows who your husband is, so you don't have to put in any effort to be found by him. Just go about your normal life, dressing the way you normally do.

2. Be respectable of others in public and in private. One of the most detestable women to men (and society alike) is a loud, abrasive woman who mistreats others. If you're in the checkout line at a restaurant speaking loudly and disrespectfully to the cashier, you've just answered your question as to why you're single. Most respectable men want a woman who won't embarrass them and knows how to

conduct herself in public. After all, you are a reflection of your husband.

3. Get rid of those gossiping, no good friends of yours. Just like we look at their friends, men often look at their potential wives' friends, and many men have ended relationships with women when they didn't like what they saw. Remember, friends are people who will come and sit in your house, influence you, influence your children and set the mood for many of the days of your life. If you're trying to bring bad friends into a good marriage, be sure to put a divorce attorney on speed dial.

4. Let the obvious huntresses wear fitted clothes, but a secret weapon for a Godly woman is the covering of her body. Sure, you can go out there half-naked and come home with twenty-five phone numbers every night for thirty days, but another

woman can go out and get one number in that time, and she'd be at the altar faster than you. Only one number is going to matter. The rest are just bedroom buddy applicants who want to rent you for a few days, a few months, a few years and sometimes, even for a lifetime. But know this: A lifetime with the wrong man is like serving life in a maximum security prison with no possibility of parole while sharing a cell with a lunatic.

5. Stop gossiping and stay out of other folk's business. Gossip reflects insecurity in a woman, and most men aren't attracted to insecure women.

6. Build your knowledge, not your shoe collection. I understand how you feel. I happen to be a woman who loves shoes too, but I love knowledge more. When a man marries you, he's going to spend a lot of time talking

with you. If the only thing you're knowledgeable about is shoes, you might as well pick out the pair you're going to wear to divorce court.

7. Never present yourself as overly confident. Sure, men like confidence, but there is a difference between confidence and conceit. At the same time, many women who present themselves as overly confident have low self-perception, and men know this. Just be yourself.

8. Spend more money decorating your home than you do yourself. Your husband is looking to build his life with you, and when he sees that you are trying to make your home a better place, this tells him that it would be nice to have a home with you. An overly decorated woman with a messy home is like a Christmas in July: she's useless.

9. Don't give a man everything he needs

to know about you. Don't tell anyone everything about you. A man is a hunter, because GOD created him that way. When he has something to hunt, he remains interested. When he knows everything there is to know about you, there is nothing left for him to hunt in you. Don't worry. Once you're married, GOD will continue to add a mystery to you as long as you stay busy in HIM. HE understands how HE created man, and HE knows that your husband needs the thrill of the chase to keep him running after you.

10.   Put GOD first at all times, and never be ashamed of HIM. A worldly man isn't truly interested in building a life with a Godly woman. A worldly man simply gets curious and wants to explore different types of women. But a wise man is so attracted to GOD that when he sees HIM in you, he will automatically be attracted to you.

Commonly Asked Questions

In this section, I am going to feature ten commonly asked questions, as well as give an answer to each question.

1. **I truly desire to be married, but it seems as if GOD is taking forever to send my husband. What should I do? I'm getting impatient.**

   Answer: The answer is simple. Find out why you are having trouble waiting. Oftentimes, an anxious woman is fueled by a void; a void in which the LORD wants to fill. Go before the LORD and empty your heart out to HIM. Tell HIM those hidden truths that you are afraid to share with HIM and then ask HIM to clean you up and fill those voids. Remember, the WORD tells us to be anxious for nothing. There's a reason for this. When we're anxious, we often overlook the obvious because we become intently focused on what we want and not what we need. While you are waiting on GOD to send Mr. Right, get busy in purpose. Find out what you are supposed to be doing and do it. Everyone has a GOD-given assignment, but the majority of people don't fulfill it because they are too busy focusing on their own desires. Read your Bible more, go to church more and do those things GOD told you to do. In other words, get busy in purpose. In due season, you will reap if you do not faint.

2. **Everyone says to wait, but why should I wait for my husband?**
Answer: Go outside and plant a flower in the winter time and the seed will likely die. The season for growth is oftentimes spring, and

anything planted out of season will not grow unless it can withstand the climate of the area it's in. GOD doesn't allow a spring flower to grow in winter because winter conditions would kill that flower. You too are a flower in bloom, but there is a season when you'll be ready to be picked by your husband. If GOD allowed you to go into the next season unprepared, your marriage wouldn't survive. In the wait, GOD is actually protecting you. Additionally, we oftentimes prolong our own waits because of our thinking patterns. For example, if you find yourself anxious to be married, that's indicative of a soul tie being present in your life or a void being present in your life. GOD wants to sever those soul ties and fill those voids before HE sends your husband to you. Why is this? Because whatever man HE gives HIS daughters to is favored by HIM; therefore, HE doesn't want to punish HIS sons by giving them women who haven't bloomed into who they are yet. When a flower has bloomed, it is then that it can be picked. The average woman hasn't sown the seeds of faithfulness to begin the process of being rooted in the WORD and growing up in the Truth. Because of this, many single women wait aimlessly, and they watch others who haven't waited as long as they have get married. What they didn't understand was those women finally surrendered to GOD, gave up on themselves and just let GOD plant them in the right places at the right time. HE is our CREATOR. HE knows what we need, when we need it and where we need to be.

3. **Sometimes, I truly want to just marry an ex of mine who I know**

loves me. I believe we could make it work. What are your takes on this?

Answer: An ex is an ex for a reason. If I took a chalkboard and put five minus five on the board, and told you to answer it, what would your answer be? What if I placed five answers on the board and told you to strike out every answer that was incorrect? You strike out every number except zero, which of course, is the correct answer. But somehow, you start to question yourself. Maybe if you took five straws out of one hand and placed them in the other hand, you'd still have five straws. They've just switched hands. So, you go and change your answer to five. You get a failing grade and the next day, you're faced with that question again. The teacher looks like she's in a better mood than yesterday, so your answer is five yet again. The teacher still says you're wrong. That's how relationships work. No matter how you cut it, Mr. Wrong is just not right for you, and even though you can make it work in your mind, you won't be able to make it work in your life. You can reason with yourself many ways, and you can come up with some pretty good justifications as to why you should give Mr. Wrong another shot. Nevertheless, once it's all said and done, you'll still find yourself arriving at the same conclusion: GOD said that man was the wrong answer, and no matter how you cut it, HE'S not going to change HIS mind. Mr. Wrong can never be Mr. Right. Anytime you return to a man from your past, you are basically saying that you're still not convinced he's the wrong man and you need a little more heartbreak to convince you.

4. **A man came up to me and told me that GOD said I am his wife. What should I do? I do like him.**

   Answer: Beware of wolves in sheep's clothing. This is a common snare for single, Christian women. This trap was set by the enemy, and is designed to play on a woman's faith and fear. You see, when you truly believe the man who spoke those words is a man of GOD, you will feel conflicted as to how you should answer him. You don't want to tell him no because you're worried about displeasing GOD. At the same time, you aren't really sure if GOD said you were that man's wife or not. Here's the answer to that: He's not your husband unless GOD says otherwise. I've met countless single women who've been approached by men in that very manner, and many of them were confused because they respected the men who spoke those words. This is especially true if they know or believe the man to be a true man of GOD. But one thing you have to remember is that even a real prophet can tell a lie. Just because GOD uses a man doesn't mean the devil can't turn around and use that same man. As a matter of fact, Satan sets out to use men and women of GOD because people respect and trust them. Pray about that man and ask the LORD to reveal who he is to you. In the meantime, do not speak with that man until you've gotten a Word from Heaven as to who he is to you. If you open up yourself to speak with him often, he'll look for ways to get into your heart, and once he's there, you'll believe what you want to believe because receiving the truth means your heart has to be broken.

5. **You said you won't kiss before**

marriage. Is kissing a sin, and where can I find scripture to back that up?

Answer: The Bible never said that kissing is a sin, however, we must understand that the men and women of old did not kiss before marriage. Kissing before marriage has become a western culture, and we've been taught that it's not only okay, but it's expected. What happens when you kiss a man? It's simple. You warm up his oven and he sets a fire in your lamp. Before you know it, your flesh is burning with desire, and it's easy to fall into temptation when this happens. Why kiss every man who gets past your discernment? Don't you realize that many Ishmaels will ask you out and pretend to be Isaac? Would you have it that you kissed all of them because they did a good job in mimicking Isaac? Do you want Mr. Right to find you with a cold sore and a prescription? Soul ties are established through communications and kissing, even though sex often births the strongest soul ties. Anything that causes your flesh to burn is causing you to sin against GOD. Even thinking about sex is a sin, and this is evidenced in the scriptures. You can kiss as much as you want, but know this: GOD will never send the right man until you learn to keep your lips and your body in holiness. HE is not going to send a man to you if you are going to cause that man to stumble.

6. **I have a male friend who's interested in me. He's Christian and he truly loves the LORD, but when we're together, we often slip up and have sex. Can't we just get married to make it right or did having sex with him ruin any chances of us ever having a successful marriage?**

Answer: GOD is the head of CHRIST, CHRIST is the head of man, and man is the head of woman. CHRIST leads us to GOD, and a husband leads his wife in CHRIST to GOD. If a man is not leading you in the direction of righteousness, he is leading you in the direction of unrighteousness. If he's not leading you towards GOD, he's leading you away from HIM. That's a clear indication that he is not the promised husband. He is a counterfeit. By marrying the counterfeit, you delay or cancel Mr. Right's arrival in your life. Additionally, the marriage could possibly work, but if you knew what you'd have to go through to make it work, you'd wait on GOD. One thing about the imagination is it shows you the fun you can have, but it can't comprehend the pain you'll endure with the wrong man. Again, I've been down that road twice, and what I've learned is: There is no blessing in sin, and anytime you go into sin to get a man, you'll come out with a sinner.

7. **I told a man that I was celibate, and I will never have sex before marriage. After that, he stopped calling me. I really like him, and I do believe he's a great catch. What should I do?**
Answer: What should you do?
Rejoice in the LORD. The WORD did what it was supposed to do...it drove that devil away from you. Meditate on James 4:7, which reads, "Submit yourselves therefore to God. Resist the devil, and he will flee from you." Be sure to keep thanking GOD for delivering you and showing you James 4:7 in action. You like what you see, and you like what he's said, but you wouldn't like what he'll take you through if you were to give in to him. Refusing to sin will drive many

men away from you, but that's okay; they weren't supposed to be anywhere near you anyway. When you refused to sin, you were basically saying to Satan that if he were to let you take his son and marry him, you'd introduce him to righteousness, and Satan won't have that. He needs you to give him a sin offering so his son can lead you into darkness. Don't call that man. Leave that man and that situation alone and continue to wait on GOD for your GOD-sent husband. Don't accept anyone as your husband just because you like them. Wait on GOD so HE can give you a testimony that bears witness to how much HE loves you.

8. **Everyone talks about Ruth, Boaz, Ishmael and Isaac. How do they relate to single Christian women?**
Answer: Ruth's husband died, and her mother in law told her to go back to

the land she was from. Instead of going back like her sister-in-law, Ruth stayed with Naomi (her mother-in-law) and continued to follow Jewish custom. She obeyed wise counsel, and because of this, she was eventually married to Boaz. The lesson of Ruth is used to show single women how wise counsel can lead their Boaz to them. Boaz represents a redeemer; someone who comes along and pays the price for another person. Because Ruth had been married before, she was not a virgin, but a widow. In that time, the kinsmen redeemer would take the widow and make her his wife, but it was no secret: widows weren't always looked upon favorably, and many weren't redeemed. Instead, they remained widows all of their lives. Boaz redeemed Ruth, and the Bible tells us they went on to have a child together. Women often refer to Christian men who find them in their fields (work, lack and obedience) as their Boaz because they believe these men have come to rescue them. As for Ishmael and Isaac, Ishmael represents the works of the flesh; whereas, Isaac represents the promises of GOD. GOD told Abraham (then Abram) that HE would bless him to be the father of many nations, but as the Bible states, Sarah (then Sarai) thought she was too old to conceive, so she sent Abraham to sleep with her maidservant, Hagar. Hagar conceived a son, and his name was Ishmael. Ishmael represents the works of the flesh and unbelief. Because of Sarah's doubt, she sent her husband to sleep with another woman. Eventually, Sarah did conceive a son whom she named Isaac, and Isaac represents the promises of GOD. GOD honored HIS words and gave Abraham a son through his wife. Therefore, Ishmael is often used to represent the man who is not sent as the promise, but the man who comes as the result of a woman's unbelief. He represents the works of the flesh. Isaac represents the promise; the man who comes as a result of our faith and perseverance.

9. **How can I tell if a man is my GOD-appointed husband or not?**
Answer: Sometimes, GOD will place an alarm in you that will warn you over and over again that the man you are courting is not your husband. Most women ignore this alarm and proceed with the man of their dreams. They try to silence this alarm by asking their Ishmaels pointed questions. For example, many women can sense or spiritually discern that the man they are

courting has wandering eyes, hands, feet and so on. But because they want to continue in the relationship with the man, they simply tell him what they feel, and they open up their hearts for whatever answer he gives. They know he's going to lie, but they've already decided to welcome in that lie for the sake of continuing in that relationship. One of the best ways to tell if he's your husband is not invite him into your life to play any sort of romantic role with you. No holding hands, no kissing and no making plans for the future. You simply talk with him and lay his name at the altar of GOD, asking GOD who he is to you. Also ask the LORD to run that man off if he is not GOD'S selected husband for you. By doing this, you will cause the man in question to be tried by fire if he is not the GOD-sent husband. He may find himself getting more and more anxious to kiss you, hold you or touch you. When you don't give in, he will stop pursuing you because he can't lead you into sin. One of the easiest ways to tell if a man is an Ishmael is to refuse to sin with him and to refuse to allow him to tempt you with sin. Any devil sent your way requires a sin offering to continue with you.

10.   **Why is having sex before marriage wrong? I find it hard to believe that a loving GOD would punish me for doing something that HE created.**

Answer: Contrary to popular belief, there is no such thing as sex before marriage. Fornication means to illegally engage in a sexual act with someone who has not committed themselves to GOD to act as your husband. It means that the man

350

uncovers you without spiritually covering you. By having sex with you, that man illegally marries you, but he wasn't given your FATHER'S permission to have you. In this, he becomes your husband, but because the foundation of your marriage is not CHRIST, your marriage is illegal. Fornication is an act of the flesh, and the Bible warns us to not be led of our flesh, because the desires of our flesh lead to death.

Your desire to fornicate stems from past relationships in which you've engaged in sexual activity. With women, it often means your soul recognizes you as a married woman; therefore, your body responds accordingly. Once you repent and submit your body wholly to GOD, asking GOD to divorce you from the men of your past, you will find that those sexual cravings will slowly fade away as those soul ties are broken. In those cases where you are dealing with a spirit of perversion, those desires may not fade, but fasting should break that spirit's stronghold on your mind.

Sex before marriage is wrong because the woman is left exposed, not the man. The man is the head of the woman, so he can easily walk away because CHRIST is the head of the man. An uncovered woman is exposed to the realm of the demonic, and for every man you've slept with, there is something that occurred in you that slowly brought you downward. That's why you'll find that women who've been promiscuous tend to be louder, distrusting and more combative. The souls of many men are in them, and until the LORD severs those soul ties, they won't be whole again. In the

Bible is the story of a Levite who went to retrieve his concubine from her father's house. While staying there, some men from that town surrounded his father-in-law's house and demanded that his father-in-law send him out so they could have sex with him. The father-in-law pleaded with them to not do the evil they were set on doing, and he offered them his virgin daughter. The scriptures tell us that the men took the woman, raped and abused her all night long. In the morning, she was found at the doorstep of her father's house deceased. He then put her on his donkey, took her home and cut her body up into twelve pieces. He sent each piece of her body throughout the twelve tribes of Israel. What he did was symbolic of the evils that was going on in Israel. It also symbolized how divided that one woman had become because of the rape she'd endured. The point he wanted to make was how divided Israel had become. A woman who is full of soul ties is divided in herself. A house divided will not stand, and a double-minded man is unstable in all his ways. The Bible tells us that a wife's desire is to please her husband. Whenever a woman has multiple husbands, she becomes unstable because her soul wasn't designed to be linked to multiple souls. She was designed for one man, and anytime we operate outside of our design, we will slowly self destruct.

When GOD commanded that we do not fornicate, HE didn't say that to challenge us; HE said it to protect us. GOD knows how a woman is designed. After all, HE designed her. GOD knows that if a woman starts engaging in fornication many men will

come along and try her own, but
refuse to buy her. Additionally, he
knows that children will be born of
these illegal unions; children in which
that man would not provide for, nor
would he teach to walk in
righteousness. In sinning against your
body, you are also sinning against
GOD, because you are agreeing to
become a conduit for Satan's works in
the earth realm. Additionally,
anytime a man sleeps with a woman,
he illegally becomes her husband,
and is obligated to provide for her
and the children he births by her. The
Bible tells us that when he doesn't
provide for his family, he is worse
than an infidel. 10. An infidel is an
unbeliever. In other words, GOD is
trying to protect that man as well.
The answer is simple: GOD told you
not to fornicate because HE loves
you, and HE knows that in obedience,

355

HE can protect you from the wages of death. In disobedience, you fall under the curse of sin, and GOD has already judged sin. HIS WORD will not return to HIM void. In other words, HE can't take HIS WORD back to protect you.

Scriptural Direction

Matthew 25:23: His lord said unto him, Well done, good and faithful servant; thou hast been faithful over a few things, I will make thee ruler over many things: enter thou into the joy of thy lord.

Note: Many women don't enter the joy of the LORD because they aren't faithful over the few things they have. How do you manage your money? Do you keep your house clean? What about your children? Are they disciplined or are they spoiled? Many women want husbands, only to bring them into chaotic situations, and they expect these men to fix their lives. You need to get your home in order and become faithful over what you do have before GOD will send you a husband. Would you want GOD to send you a husband who was in debt, living in a dirty place with his disorderly children? Well, when a man asks for his wife, I doubt if he's asking for a fixer-upper.

Romans 12:1: I beseech you therefore, brethren, by the mercies of God, that ye present your bodies a living sacrifice, holy, acceptable unto God, which is your reasonable service.

Note: The issue is that many women just don't respect their bodies. Because of this, many women engage in fornication, adultery or tempting men to lust after them. Yes, it is wrong to dress in a way that intentionally tempts a man into sin. Cover your body up, but you can still be stylish and cute with it. A well-dressed Godly woman who commands her atmosphere is irresistible to the man who's anointed to marry her.

Matthew 6:34: Take therefore no thought for the morrow: for the morrow shall take thought for the things of itself. Sufficient unto the day is the evil thereof.

Note: What are you worried about now? Many women aren't found by their husbands because they are so weighed down worrying that they will be a burden to him. Stop worrying about tomorrow. Just take each day one breath at a time. Always remember that there are many problems you'll face in this world, and those problems may present themselves as giants; nevertheless, David overcame Goliath because he trusted in the LORD. Do you?

2 Corinthians 10:5-6: Casting down imaginations, and every high thing that exalteth itself against the knowledge of God, and bringing into captivity every thought to the obedience of Christ; And having in a readiness to revenge all disobedience, when your obedience is fulfilled.

Note: What is the knowledge of GOD?

Truth, of course. GOD knows who your husband is, even when you don't. GOD knows when your season to meet your husband is, but you don't. GOD knows whether that man who's courting you is your GOD-appointed spouse or your self-appointed no-no.

Our imaginations are a very blessed place, but we often make them into prisons where we imprison ourselves to thoughts of spending our lives with men who aren't right for us. As women, we often meet men and begin to envision our lives with them. Before the week is out, we've tried on their last names, we've pictured our kids with them, and we've already traveled to a few countries with them in our imaginations. This often makes it harder to accept the truth when it is discovered that the men we've mentally married are not our husbands. Because of our imaginations, many women have ignored the obvious to pursue their dreams. Cast down those imaginations, and just worry about today. Tomorrow will worry about itself.

Matthew 22:37-40: Jesus said unto him, Thou shalt love the Lord thy God with all thy heart, and with all thy soul, and with all thy mind. This is the first and great commandment. And the second is like unto it, Thou shalt love thy neighbour as thyself. On these two commandments hang all the law and the prophets.

Note: Here's a major problem amongst many believing women: They don't love GOD with all their heart. They only love HIM with some of their heart. How can you tell the difference? GOD said that if we love HIM, we are to keep HIS commandments. Does your light shine before men? Is it obvious that you're Christian, or do you leave onlookers guessing? When you truly love the LORD, it will radiate through your person and be seen by anyone who meets you. If you don't love GOD with your whole heart, and you don't love your neighbor as you love yourself, you can't properly love a husband. You'd likely make an idol of him, or you'd make an idol of yourself and expect him to worship you. Do you feed the homeless or are they beneath you in your eyes? How do you treat others who have less than you? You see, all of this is important because it reflects whether or not you have love in you or if you are just operating in religious tolerance. A woman without love is not worthy of being called a wife.

Matthew 6:33: But seek ye first the kingdom of God, and his righteousness; and all these things shall be added unto you. **Note:** And this should be the scripture that closes the curtains. Most believing women seek a man before they seek the LORD. They try to put the LORD in the backseat to their plans, and they expect HIM to wait for HIS Name to be called. GOD is saying to seek the Kingdom of GOD first and ALL its righteousness. HE said that in doing so, HE would add all those things to you. If you seek a man first, you'll find a man, but he won't be the right man.

Ephesians 4:26-27: Be ye angry, and sin not: let not the sun go down upon your wrath: Neither give place to the devil.

Note: How many people are you still mad at? When the Bible says, "don't give place to the devil," it's talking about your heart. It's okay to be angry sometimes, but those issues need to be addressed and resolved before the close of each day. A woman who stores up anger is one the Bible warns against. Proverbs 21:9 reads, "It is better to dwell in a corner of the housetop, than with a brawling woman in a wide house." Proverbs 27:15 reads, "A continual dropping in a very rainy day and a contentious woman are alike." Proverbs 21:19 reads, "It is better to dwell in the wilderness, than

with a contentious and an angry woman."
This is a serious issue. Lay all of your sins,
hurts and anger at the altar. Despite what
mainstream television tells you, no man is
going to come and rescue you from your
pain. Your husband needs to find that
you've already been saved by the LORD, and
the shell-shock you've suffered from your
past relationships is a thing of the past.

Matthew 5:16: Let your light so shine
before men, that they may see your good
works, and glorify your Father which is in
heaven.

Note: I went to Walmart one day, and I'd
found a really good parking place. I waited
for the vehicle to finish moving out of the
parking space, and as it was backing out, I
noticed a vehicle behind me had started
going around me. This isn't unusual when a
person simply wants to go to another aisle,
but the man who was backing out didn't
leave room for anyone to go anywhere. I

then noticed that the driver was beginning to position the car to take that parking space, so I drove up on the tail of the vehicle that was moving out to keep them from taking my spot. Suddenly, I heard screaming and I looked to my left to see a woman hanging out of the passenger's side of the car that had attempted to slyly take that parking place. She was screaming, and I quote, "We ain't want that parking space boo-boo! We ain't want that parking space!" I immediately became disgusted with her, and I frowned at her. I was on my phone with a friend, and before I realized it, I'd yelled out that the woman was stupid. I went inside Walmart and walked around for a bit, but I was still agitated about what happened. I was clearly in my flesh. I thought to myself that if that woman was to approach me in the store, I was going to mace her and drag her to the book aisle to read a book. Suddenly, a song came on out of a little gadget sitting on the corner of that aisle, and it sang: *This little light of mine. I'm gonna let it shine. This little light of mine. I'm gonna let it shine. This little light of mine. I'm gonna let it shine. Let it shine, let it shine, let it shine.* Immediately, I dropped my head and giggled. I had to humble myself or be humiliated. I was and am a woman of GOD, and as such, I have to be careful how I conduct myself. I could have easily ended up holding a sign while the police took my snapshot just because of a parking space and a lost soul. What should I have done? I should have let them take that space. I should have ignored the woman, and I should have let that issue go immediately. The issue with many of us is that we tend to hold on to things too long. I walked around for more than fifteen minutes, still carrying the act of an obviously lost soul in my spirit. I lost my opportunity to minister to that soul because I allowed them to help me step into my flesh.

As a single woman, and a Godly woman, you have to always be aware of the tricks of the enemy. Many single women don't let their lights shine. Instead, their lights flick on and off, while others have little candles that come on every Sunday morning. We have to always conduct ourselves as CHRIST conducted HIMSELF.

James 2:9: But if ye have respect to persons, ye commit sin, and are convinced of the law as transgressors.

Note: To have respect for others is to esteem some people higher than others. This is clearly a problem with a lot of single women. I know we want husbands who can provide for us and the children they'll create with us. Truthfully, GOD won't send a husband to you who cannot provide for you. 1 Timothy 5:8 reads, "But if any provide not for his own, and especially for those of his own house, he hath denied the faith, and is worse than an infidel." You can relax in GOD and know that the husband HE sends will be a good provider, but that doesn't mean he'll be rich. Too many women turn their noses up at certain men because they think they can't give them everything they want. After they marry the wrong man, they find that they have the material things they wanted, but they did not get what they needed. How you perceive others is a reflection of your relationship (or lack thereof) with GOD. Let GOD lead you in all of your communications and dealings with people, so you don't become guilty of being a transgressor.

James 4:2: Ye lust, and have not: ye kill, and desire to have, and cannot obtain: ye fight and war, yet ye have not, because ye ask not. Ye ask, and receive not, because ye ask amiss, that ye may consume it upon your lusts.
Note: You want something, but you don't

have it. You work hard, yet you still can't possess it. You battle it out with others and study aimlessly; nevertheless, you only seem to know more things that don't benefit you. Why is this? GOD says this happens for three reasons:

- You didn't ask HIM for it.
- You decided to do the work yourself.
- You ask so you can consume it upon your own lusts.

Yet you say, "I have asked GOD to send me a husband!" What you didn't realize was that you asked the wrong question. You should have asked HIM to send you your husband. If you're not a virgin and you haven't asked GOD to sever that union between the man or men you've slept with, you already have a husband or several husbands. Then again, why is it that you want a husband right now? Many women want to be married just for the sake of having legal sex. This means that other soul ties are still very present in them, and they are trying to satisfy the lusts created by those relationships. Anytime we engage in sexual activity, we will begin to have those insatiable appetites for sex, some more than others. That's because once you have sex, you become a wife...automatically. Your soul is saying that you are married; therefore, your body asks for sex. At the same time, many women (and men) have the spirit of perversion attached to them. So the issue is, many women haven't asked GOD to send them their own husbands, and the ones who do, often ask for their husbands for the wrong reasons. Maybe they want someone to come along and help them with their bills. Maybe they want someone to cure the boredom in their life. Maybe they want someone to father their children. Every need you have is to be met by GOD before a husband comes. You cannot depend on your husband. GOD wants you to depend on HIM. When the husband comes, he is to find you settled, unmarried, at peace and full of love. He shouldn't find you dangling from your last thread of sanity, full of soul ties, agitated and full of hatred.

Ask GOD for what you want, but be sure to ask in the right spirit. At the same time, please understand that anytime we ask GOD for something, HE begins to rearrange our lives to receive whatever we've asked HIM for. If you've asked to meet your GOD-appointed husband, you will likely see some of your friends fall away from you, some of your familiar relationships will end, you may be relocated, and your faith may be challenged. Here's the thing. It's not that you're being attacked; you're being prepared to receive. Don't try to stop the process, don't abort your blessing, and don't complain about what's going on. Take the time out to bless the Name of the LORD, and you'll get an understanding about what's going on in your life as soon as the process is complete.

Printed in Great Britain
by Amazon